Honeysuckle
Drive

"Stay Lit"

♡ -amy
Bowdoin

* Psalm
18:28

TULSA

ISBN 978-1-957262-56-7 (Paperback)

Yorkshire Publishing
4613 E. 91ˢᵗ St,
Tulsa, OK 74137
www.YorkshirePublishing.com
918.394.2665

Printed in the USA

Honeysuckle
Drive

Where stories aren't just told, they're lived

A 12 Week Devotional For Any Season

AMY BOWDOIN

Dedication

To all those who feel broken—

But, especially to my husband,

Who chose to love me in spite of my brokenness.

Honorable Mentions

(Who am I kidding? I LOVE these heifers!)

Amber Wigley: Incredibly talented and oh, so crafty (she drew my cover illustration), salt of the earth, genuine, honest and kind, a true giver without asking for anything in return, anyone will eat cake with you, but will they drive you to a scary doctor's appointment? She will.

Veronica Welch: Dependable, champion of the underdog, she saw something in me when I didn't see it in myself, she wrote radio stations, she made goodie bags and passed them out at church craft fairs to get my name out there, she's shared every single post I've ever written, you will not find a bigger cheerleader

Sharon Wright Mitchell: My introverted friend, she was the first one to encourage me to publish my stories, she would leave submission forms on my desk at school, she edited this entire devotional as a favor to me, she gave me constant encouragement, she's a creative published poet, look her up on Instagram: apoetseyeview!

Contents

Week 12: Revival

Preface

When I was younger—much younger—I could see angels hovering at the foot of my bed as I tried to fall asleep. I would often call my mom to my room and ask her, "Can you see them, too?" She never could, but she always believed me. That probably should have been my first sign that God had an interest in me.

My mom had me at church every Sunday morning and every Wednesday night. I don't think I ever missed a choir practice, either. I was also front row at every church lock-in, every church revival, and every vacation Bible school. When it came to church, I was there and participating. But, none of that would have been possible without a congregation who believed in planting seeds in its youth. Tabernacle Baptist Church in Carrollton, Georgia, was that church for me.

I can remember our youth minister telling us each Wednesday night that we were all born with a gift. I used to ponder—for hours—what my gift might be. It was so obvious for others. Some were born with amazing pipes. Those jokers could sing. Others were athletic, artistic, or great public speakers. I was none of those things. He did always say it might take some of us longer to figure it out. I had no idea he meant 46 YEARS.

It was the first day of 7th grade that would change my life. There was a new boy sitting at the end of our cafeteria table, and I thought he was kinda cute. I walked over and asked him if he had a girlfriend. He didn't. So, I asked him if he wanted one. And, guess what? He did. And, that's how it started… Bill and Amy.

He SWEARS he knew that very first day in 7th grade that he was gonna marry me. And, I sorta believe him. We dated forever… until

I got the big head and wanted to try my luck with older boys. It landed me a boyfriend who was in college. Bill was still a very active presence in my life. He'd ride to where we were all hanging out just to make sure this new boyfriend was treating me right. It was our senior year in high school, when I became pregnant (and married), that Bill realized he had to let me go. That would be the last time I saw him for 15 years.

At some point during those 15 years, my life spiraled outta control. Bad decisions were the only things I could make. My panic attacks were so damn crippling that they were affecting my job. If I'm honest, they were affecting everything. (My mom just spit out her coffee. She hates when I use ugly words, but sometimes that's all that captures the magnitude of a moment.) I wanted to drive my car off a bridge to make it all go away, which I don't recommend you saying out loud unless you want an extended stay in a mental hospital—which I got.

That extended stay required a leave from work. The facility confiscated all cell phones and monitored you while you slept. I can vividly remember whispering to myself, "So, this is what rock bottom looks like." But, guys, it was the most monumental month of my life. Why? That's where I found Jesus. That's where all those seeds that had been planted from my youth started to take root and multiply. I was discharged from that facility a warrior… but a warrior on a lot of pills. Who knew it took so much just to feel normal? But, it was what I needed at that time.

It was at that same time, when Bill walked back into my life. We were planning our 15 year class reunion and somehow started trading emails. I'm pretty sure it was about the passing of his sweet mom. Those emails turned into text messages and late night phone calls. I was going through a divorce, moving out, and quite the basket case. He didn't seem to mind. He's always liked a good challenge.

His pickup line at our class reunion was, "I've been waiting for you. I knew you'd come back to me." That might be the smoothest pickup line ever spoken. He had never married, so his words seemed true. I would visit him at his house the next weekend. He had a wooden box under his bed filled with all my pictures. But, that's not even the best part. He also had a red duffle bag filled to the rim with every letter I'd ever written to him. So, when he says he knew I was the one in 7th grade, I kinda believe him.

We started seeing each other every other weekend. During that time, my life returned to normal—a good normal. I give Midway Church in Carrollton, Georgia, credit for that. At that time, they offered a Saturday evening service, which I loved attending. They also offered a weekly small group class for newly divorced moms. Those two events kept me at the church twice a week. While there, I rededicated my life to Jesus and got baptized again. It was at that moment, when I came up outta that water, that I could finally breathe. It was at that moment when I knew—without a doubt—Jesus saved me.

By that summer, Bill and I were getting married. It would be his first rodeo, but I had a little practice. I'd love to say it was all roses, but it wasn't. He inherited some damaged goods. I was still slightly broken. Giant insecurities will do that to you. But, guys, he nursed me back to health… with his time, with his words of affirmation, and with his actions. He poured life-giving water into my dry well. Pills are no longer needed when your spirit finally finds peace. He held my hands and prayed for me. He left thousands of positive post-it notes around our house for me to find. He would text me sweet messages through-out my day. He still does. I can vividly remember slow dancing with him, in the dark, as I cried. He held me close and stroked my hair. It's a moment I'll never forget. He's the gentle strength the Lord knew I needed. Bill has never let me settle or play small with my life. He is my biggest cheerleader and my #1 accountability partner. He is my rock and my soulmate. But, what is his greatest attribute? He never saw me as broken. In his eyes, I've always been beautiful.

I've known fear.
I've known shame.

I've known doubt.
I've known defeat.
I've known regret.

But…

I now know forgiveness.
I now know amazing grace.
I now know sweet redemption.
AND, I finally know my gift.
It's sharing Jesus with others.

He turned my struggles into strength. He turned my mess into a powerful message. There's no such thing as too broken with Jesus. Even our pain has a purpose. You better believe it, folks. I'm living proof.

*   *   *

"We know that in all things God works for the good of those who love him, who have been called according to his purpose." Romans 8:28

*   *   *

Warning!

Have you ever walked into a room and forgot why you were there?

Have you ever looked for your glasses while they're on your head?

Have you ever forgotten something while shopping at the grocery store?

Have you ever misplaced your cell phone?

If you don't write it down, is it often forgotten?

If you answered YES to any question listed above, you need to place a pencil with this devotional. After each story and scripture, there are a few questions for you to answer. This is a must! You don't get better at math by working the problems in your head. You've gotta show your work. This same principle applies to your walk with Jesus. Writing something down is the first step towards making something happen. Don't shortchange yourself (or Jesus) by taking shortcuts.

*   *   *

"Don't just listen to God's word. You must do what it says. Otherwise, you are only fooling yourselves." James 1:22

*   *   *

Letting Go

Clutter... done. Extra weight and love handles... gone. Trash, laundry, and dirty dishes... goodbye. I have no problem letting go of things that bring me little joy. But yet, here I sit, choosing to hold on to the things that weigh me down the most: regret, old friendships, grudges, the opinions of others. Why do we do this? Better yet, why do we lay our burdens at God's feet and arise the next morning just to take them all back? It's because letting go requires an enormous amount of faith.

Dear Lord, fill my heart with faith. Fill my heart with endless confidence in your promises. Help me to hold firmly to your word. Drown out Satan's lies. You are faithful and you'll never let me fall. In Jesus's name, Amen.

PRAYER JOURNAL

Who will you pray for this week? What situations need God's guidance? Where does Jesus need to intervene? How can the Holy Spirit help? Date it and state it! Pray for these things each day this week. Update it as needed.

Day #1

Rock Bottom

Once upon a time, I was not this happy.

I was filled with waves of negative emotions: anxiety, fear, sadness, dread. It was awful. What made it even worse was that my closest friends, family and coworkers couldn't see it. They had no idea I was battling such demons until it was too late.

When we're injured on the outside, people are so kind and patient with us. They hold open doors. They offer to carry our bags. They cook us dinner. They send flowers. They bend over backwards to help us. All that changes when we're injured on the inside. All of a sudden, people expect you to just snap out of it. They even question your feelings: "Look at your life. How could you possibly be depressed?"

I don't fault the masses in their thinking. Visible wounds are easier to understand. In their defense, no amount of support would have fixed my struggles. I needed medical attention, and even knowing this, I still found it hard to accept.

> "What will people say? What will I do about my job?"

Fortunately, my momma had my back. She asked me, "What would they say or do if this were a heart attack or a stroke? They'd expect you to get immediate medical attention and not return until you're back to 100%, so that's what you're going to do." So, I took leave from work and my mother and ex-husband drove me to Atlanta to a mental health hospital that would become my home for the next month. I could have been the poster child for "Rock Bottom," folks, but don't let rock bottom fool you. It was heavenly.

I met some of the greatest, strongest people, whose burdens were far heavier than mine. I also learned some life-saving coping strategies that I still use today. It was also during this time that I fell in love with Jesus. I had been baptized. I attended church. I said my prayers. But, my relationship with Him was never like this. He loved me when I couldn't even love myself. He picked up all my broken pieces and molded me into something more. What I thought was a cage had been a cocoon all along!

> "A season of loneliness and isolation is when the caterpillar gets its wings."

Like I said before, once upon a time, I was not this happy, but falling in love with Jesus changed all that. But, in order to fall, I first had to let go.

*   *   *

*"In my distress, I called upon the Lord; to my
God I cried for help. From his temple
he heard my voice, and my cry to him reached his ears." Psalm 18:6*

*   *   *

What's weighing you down?

_____
_____
_____
_____
_____
_____

What do you need to let go of so God can lift you up?

_____
_____
_____
_____
_____
_____

Why is "letting go and letting God" so hard to do?

_____
_____
_____
_____
_____
_____

Day #2

Knox

Y'all, sometimes I even shock myself.

This dog. His name is Knox, and he's been mine for six years now.

We didn't start out this way.

I kept him fed and occasionally rubbed his head. That was it.

In my defense, I never had a pet growing up, so all those warm fuzzies were not naturally there for me. I was more worried about muddy paw prints, excessive dog hair, and what could be crawling in his fur. It wigged me out, folks, so he was not allowed in the house.

I know what you're thinking. I'm a terrible person, but I just didn't know. I didn't know how much Knox loved me or how much I needed him until my husband had to put down his dog. They had been the best of companions for over 13 years. It was heartbreaking to witness. But, that loss taught me a mighty big lesson.

Knox now goes hiking with me, camping with me, and even sleeps in the house. When he's riding in my backseat and drooling all over the door handle, my right eye only twitches a little bit. What did you expect? A miracle?

But, the part I really want you to stew on is this: WHY?!?!

Why do we have to experience a loss to appreciate what we have?

It took a failed marriage for me to truly value the sanctity of that commitment. I'm a much better spouse now because I've loved and lost.

It took my two older boys leaving the nest for me to truly grasp how quickly time flies by. I'm a much better mother now because I know—without a doubt—it won't be like this for long.

> It took the loss of a pet.
> It took leaving my hometown.
> It took resigning from a job.
> It took losing a friend.

And, some of y'all know all too well the heartache that comes with losing a parent.

Oh, the things we'd do differently if we could!

One of the hardest lessons in life is letting go.

It can't be taught.

It must be felt.

Don't forget what you learn.

*   *   *

> *"Keep putting into practice all you learned and*
> *received from me—everything you heard*
> *from me and saw me doing. Then the God of*
> *peace will be with you." Philippians 4:9*

*   *   *

What lessons did you have to learn the hard way?

_____

_____

_____

_____

_____

_____

What #1 life lesson would you be willing to share with others?

_____

_____

_____

_____

_____

_____

How have you used these lessons to be a better person?

_____

_____

_____

_____

_____

_____

Day #3

The Second Hug

Like any good mama, I always kiss my family goodbye. And, like any good family, they always kiss me back. But, one day, a little boy followed me to the car for one final hug. I thought it was a sweet gesture and one of those one-and-done kinda things. Nope! He has done it again and again and again. Just when I think he's over it and not coming, our garage door swings open and there he is.

Just last night I kissed him goodbye. He was chillaxin' on the couch and I was headed to Zumba. Before I could turn on my car, he was squeezing my neck. That's the good stuff, folks.

"I can't let you leave without your second hug."

And, I'm not even gonna lie. That "second hug" is much sweeter than the first. That "second hug" takes effort and thoughtfulness. That "second hug" proves I'm loved and I'm important. That "second hug" makes me feel mighty special. That "second hug" is my favorite.

Sometimes love needs a second chance. It's the best gift in life. That's exactly what Jesus gave you when he died on that cross. What an opportunity! Don't waste it, folks.

*　　*　　*

"The faithful love of the Lord never ends!
His mercies never cease. They are
new every morning; great is your faithfulness." Lamentations 3:2-3

*　　*　　*

Who in your life needs a second chance?

_____

_____

_____

_____

_____

_____

What must you "let go of" to make this happen?

_____

_____

_____

_____

_____

_____

Why is it so hard to let go of bitterness?

_____

_____

_____

_____

_____

_____

Name two people who would love one of your hugs right now:

_____

_____

_____

Day #4

Speak Up

I've been there.

I've been defeated, discouraged, and depressed. *You're gonna be okay.*

I've been frustrated, angry, and bitter. *You're gonna be okay.*

I've been scared, filled with doubt, and exhausted. *You're gonna be okay.*

I've been hurt, searching for answers, and questioning God. *You're gonna be okay.*

Let me repeat that for the folks in the back. *YOU'RE GONNA BE OKAY!*

I've been writing daily for a while now, and if I've learned anything, it's this: we have more in common than we admit. And, it's that admitting that's the hard part.

That sneaky devil is quite good at his job. He makes us feel isolated and all alone, like we're the only ones experiencing a problem. He shames us into silence—a silence that further separates us from friends, family, help, and God. What a jerk-face!

If I don't tell anyone, it will be okay. *False.*

If I ignore it, it will go away. *False.*

If they know, it will only make it worse. *False.*

If I share my feelings, they won't like me anymore. *False.*

Guys, don't believe Satan's lies. Just because you're struggling doesn't mean you're failing.

I promise talking things over is a much better solution than throwing it all away. Speak up—even if your voice shakes. And know you are NEVER alone. I've been there. She's been there. He's been there. They've been there. Everybody's been there.

You've got this. And, **you're gonna be okay**.

* * *

"She is clothed with strength and dignity, and she laughs without fear of the future." Proverbs 31:25

* * *

What's your biggest fear?

_____

_____

_____

_____

_____

_____

_____

Would you ever share this fear with others? Why or why not?

_____

_____

_____

_____

_____

_____

Explain the difference between struggling and failing.

_____

_____

_____

_____

_____

_____

Where are you struggling?

_____

_____

_____

_____

_____

_____

Amy Bowdoin

Where are you failing?

_____

_____

_____

_____

_____

_____

What are you gonna do about it?

_____

_____

_____

_____

_____

_____

Day #5

Dead Limbs

I'm a people person, so naturally I want people to like me. If you ever met my daddy, no other explanation would be needed. The social butterfly gene runs deeply in our DNA. But, I tried to be friends with some folks once, and it just didn't work out.

I'd love to say this was in middle school or high school, but it wasn't. It was actually just a couple years ago. It was awkward. It was forced—much like trying to fit a square peg in a round hole. My hubby noticed it before I did. He kept telling me, "You need to cut bait," but I've always been stubborn. Eventually I realized my "friends" and I weren't headed in the same direction. I also realized the only way to win with toxic people is not to play.

It felt good to walk away, but I also felt like a failure. Jesus loves EVERYONE, but these heifers were getting on my last nerve. How did He do it? But then it hit me. Yes, Jesus was kind, respectful, compassionate, and courteous to EVERYONE. But, He only welcomed twelve (disciples) into his tribe. Think about that for a minute, folks.

Growth always involves some pruning. Being married to a landscaper has taught me that. So, when God prunes your branches, let those dead limbs fall! You can't be who God is calling you to be and hold on to the same old habits and friendships. Beautiful growth would be stunted if God didn't remove the very things that hinder it.

It's time you branch out.

*   *   *

*"He cuts off every branch in me that bears no
fruit, while every branch that does
bear fruit he prunes so that it will be even more fruitful." John 15:2*

*   *   *

Describe a time when you had to walk away from a friend.

_____

_____

_____

_____

_____

_____

How did you know it wasn't the right fit?

_____

_____

_____

_____

_____

_____

What other areas of your life could use some pruning?

_____

_____

_____

_____

_____

_____

_____

Day #6

Rotten Fruit

We've all heard the old adage, "One bad apple spoils the whole bunch." And, if you don't think that's true, you need to get out more.

All it takes is one.

One negative person who…

> Spews venom
> Is always so combative
> Only sees problems
> Constantly whines
> Constantly complains
> Constantly disagrees
> Constantly questions
> Constantly refuses to bend

And, here's the crazy thing. I've discovered I'm highly allergic to this type of person. When I'm in their presence, my right foot starts tapping, my blood pressure starts boiling, and my eyes start rolling. I can't even hide it. There's not enough Benadryl at CVS to alleviate my allergic reaction to negative people.

We have a strict rule at our house.

Say it once, it's a statement.

Say it twice, you're officially complaining.

If you say it three (or more) times, you're whining… and no whining is allowed.

Unfortunately, this rule doesn't work as well with other family members, friends, coworkers, or acquaintances. So, what do we do?

I kinda wanna be like Jesus when he cleansed the temple. You know, just start flipping tables and really shake things up. But, guess what? If I do that, the devil wins. I've allowed that one bad apple to taint my sweet spirit. Even in the Garden of Eden, it was never just the apple. It was always the "pair." So, how do we handle difficult people? How do we keep from joining their negativity?

I ALWAYS refer back to Michelle Obama and Will Smith. I bet you didn't see that one coming. But, they penned my two favorite phrases of all time.

"When they go low, we go high." We're gonna be very intentional and rise above their toxicity. And, we're also gonna "Let God deal with the things they do cause hate in our heart will consume us, too." There's no need to respond. There's no need to worry or seek revenge. Rotten fruit will fall by itself! Amen! (My sweet friend Rachel taught me that.)

And, while it only takes one bad apple to ruin the whole bunch, it only took one Savior to save the whole world. One person, folks.

That's the power of one.

> One smile
> One kind word
> One look
> One invitation
> One chance
> One shot
> One sacrifice
> One more try
> One spark

"What YOU do makes a difference. But, you have to decide what kinda difference you wanna make." Be a fountain not a drain, folks.

Today's goal: There's a big difference between ignoring and overcoming. Stay focused on Jesus. He's the one!

*　　*　　*

"There is salvation in no one else! God has given no other name under heaven by which we must be saved." Acts 4:12

*　　*　　*

Who drains you? Why?

_____

_____

_____

_____

_____

_____

_____

Who fills you with joy? Why?

_____

_____

_____

_____

_____

_____

_____

Why is it important to know your drains from your fountains?

_____

_____

_____

_____

_____

_____

How do you make a difference to others?

_____

_____

_____

_____

_____

_____

_____

Day #7

Chase After It

I write daily devotionals and share scripture each day, so one would think I'd have faith of steel. Yet when my own faith was tested, I caved. At the first sign of trouble, I threw in the towel. [Bad mammogram after bad mammogram.] A few summers ago, I thought I was dying, and it was awful! After several biopsies, I learned that I would be okay. Thank you, Jesus! But, I never want to forget that feeling. I had this crazy intense desire to do more, to see more, to be more. All I could think about was all the things left undone, all my hopes and dreams, all those things I had put on the back burner because I thought I had more time.

The majority of my "near death" experience was created in my head, but that was all it took, folks. It changed me. I now guard my time fiercely. I'm selective with my attention. But, more than anything else, I'm courageous... and that's made all the difference. If I wanna do something, I chase after it—not next year or next month, not next week or next time. Right now! My biggest fear is running outta time, and I was reminded of this fear yesterday.

I took my youngest son to hit range balls at a nearby state park's golf course. We were second in line, waiting exactly 6 feet behind an elderly man renting a golf cart. He was clearly a regular as everyone knew his name. The golf manager even came out of his office to speak to him. It went something like this.

"Hey, Bob. I'm sorry to hear about Gene."

"They cremated him on Friday."

"Wow! It seems like he was just in here with you."

33

"He was—the Friday before he was cremated. It's so crazy. One week we're golfing partners, and the next week he's dead."

"I'm so sorry."

"He had recently turned 70, had finally retired, and had just bought himself a convertible. He had always wanted one. He was finally loving his life and then he died."

Their conversation gave me mixed emotions. Gene died loving his life. That's a blessing. But, according to his buddy Bob, it took him 70 YEARS to get there. Seventy years?!?!?! That time frame freaks me out, folks. It also reminds me to live a lot more intentionally and less outta habit.

If God has placed a desire on your heart, and it gnaws away at you, then you should probably chase after it—not next year or next month, not next week or next time. Right now! Give up what's keeping you from living your best life. Let go of what's holding you down. There's a huge difference between giving up and letting go… and it's called surrender. Stop resisting God's nudge and chase after it, folks.

*   *   *

"Trust in the Lord with all your heart and lean not on your own understanding; in all your ways submit to him, and he will make your paths straight." Proverbs 3:5-6

*   *   *

There's something gnawing at your heart right now. What is it?

_____

_____

_____

_____

_____

_____

_____

What's holding you back?

_____

_____

_____

_____

_____

_____

_____

What does surrender look like to you?

_____

_____

_____

_____

_____

_____

_____

Week Two

Awakening

Do you remember your teacher turning off the classroom lights to show a movie? Do you remember what happened when the movie was over? Some joker would always race to turn on the overhead lights and blind half the class. Awakening kinda happens just like that. It's a realization that shocks the system. Usually it takes a life lesson to get us there, but once that lesson is learned… watch out!

> *Dear Lord, the world can be a dark place. Help me to chase after your light. Fill me with strength and steadfastness. Keep me from bending to the world's demands. Be my guiding light. In Jesus's name, Amen.*

PRAYER JOURNAL

Who will you pray for this week? What situations need God's guidance? Where does Jesus need to intervene? How can the Holy Spirit help? Date it and state it! Pray for these things each day this week. Update it as needed.

_____

_____

_____

_____

_____

_____

_____

_____

_____

_____

_____

_____

_____

_____

_____

_____

_____

_____

_____

_____

_____

_____

_____

_____

Day #1

Christmas in October

I have a tiny confession to make. As I type this devotional, all my Christmas decorating is D.O.N.E! The tree, the mantel, the lighted garland on the stairs, all of it. And, YES! I'm fully aware it's October. But... I don't care.

Once upon a time, I allowed the opinions of others to dictate my schedule (I allowed that mess to dictate a lot of things actually). Because of those opinions, I would have totally waited until a more "acceptable" date AND been totally stressed out with trying to make it all happen. It's not worth it, folks.

All that unnecessary stress would have caused me to miss Hallmark moments with my own family. But, not now. We took the entire weekend to do it. We watched Christmas movies, made hot chocolate and sugar cookies, and snuggled under fuzzy blankets. It was fantastic! Joy and cheer were never meant to be rushed or packed into a small window of time. Those feelings are something you wanna savor... all weekend long.

So, now (that I'm older and wiser) I look at my schedule and what's best for MY family is what rules the roost. I know we're out of town each weekend until December. I know how I behave when I'm stressed. I also know when my oldest son flies home for Thanksgiving. When he walks through that door, I want it to be magical for him: twinkling lights, the smell of fresh cookies, the works, folks. And, there's absolutely nothing magical about a stressed-out, overworked mother.

> But, did you catch what I just said?
> I know... our schedule.

I know… what stress does to my mood.
I know… when he arrives.
I know… the feelings I want him to take back home to Philadelphia.

Guess who doesn't know these things? *The world!*
Guess who doesn't have a dog in the fight? *The world!*

Yet, all my life, I've allowed the world's opinion to dictate what I do… in my own home. That's some poppycock right there!

But, if I've learned anything in my 40s, it's this: NEVER feel guilty doing what's best for you! Never. "It takes NOTHING to join the crowd. It takes everything to stand alone." What are you standing for?

*　　*　　*

*"Don't copy the behavior and customs of this
world, but let God transform you
into a new person by changing the way you think. Then you will learn
to know God's will for you, which is good and
pleasing and perfect." Romans 12:2*

*　　*　　*

How has "the world" kept you from living your best life? What can you do to change that?

_____
_____
_____
_____
_____
_____
_____

What would you do if you didn't care about the world's opinion?

_____
_____
_____
_____
_____
_____
_____

What change do you need God's help with?

_____
_____
_____
_____
_____
_____
_____

Day #2

Highlight the Good

Man, I barely survived! What a crazy combination—a full moon AND a Friday the 13th! I believe that mess can throw you for a loop, but it's only because I'm a bigger believer in something else: IF YOU LOOK FOR IT, YOU WILL FIND IT!

My kiddos (at school) were a little more excited yesterday, but I was looking for it. The traffic in my town was awful yesterday, but I was looking for it (and it is Winder, the city of too many red lights). My order was incorrect at Taco Bell, but I was looking for it. I pitched a tent in my backyard and here comes an insane thunderstorm. I wasn't looking for that, but it definitely fit the mood of a Friday the 13th.

My hubby is out of town. It's just me and my baby boy in that tent, so I'm on high alert. It's 2 A.M. What was that? I just heard it again. I'm peeping out the window with one finger on the trigger. Silence. But, I'm a total girl and now I'm spooked, and it is a full moon. So, I wake up Bo, my youngest son, and tell him we're moving inside. We are almost at the back door, when out of nowhere, darts a giant, solid black cat. Geez, Louise! (But, that's not really what came outta my mouth.) Last night's small heart attack was brought to you courtesy of one full moon and a Friday the 13th. But, if you look for it, you will find it, folks! And, we had been looking for it—since last Saturday to be exact. That was our black cat, Chase, and he'd been missing since last Saturday. Ha!

I'm now on my 2nd cup of coffee, and Bo's still asleep. What a night! But, guys, today's lesson is much deeper than a full moon.

What do you see…

- in your friendships
- your marriage
- your family
- your coworkers
- your country
- your mirror

"It's not what you look at that matters, it's what you see." Sure, we could pinpoint flaws, list things that grate on our nerves, and place blame on others, but that route leads us straight towards defeat, discouragement, division, and divorce. NOTHING thrives under a microscope—especially our relationships. Train your mind to highlight the good stuff. The smallest change in perspective can make all the difference.

* * *

"Teach me what I cannot see; if I have done wrong, I will not do it again." Job 34:32

* * *

What do you see when you look in the mirror? Who are you when the world's not looking?

_____

_____

_____

_____

_____

_____

_____

What "good stuff" are you not seeing?

_____

_____

_____

_____

_____

_____

_____

Day #3

Like a Boss

So, my parents spent the weekend with us, and we had a great time. I was able to bask in the sunshine while spending all afternoon blabbing with my daddy. I get my non-stop talking gene from him, so our afternoon was rich in conversation.

At one point, we reminisced about all the words of wisdom he's shared with me over the years. One of my favorites is "tan fat is prettier than white fat." So, he sat under the shade of the umbrella and had me roasting in the sun.

He's got some good tidbits though. "Never take advice from someone you wouldn't trade places with." So simple, yet filled with so much truth. But, the one that has always stuck with me is this: "Notice what successful people do and do that." Kinda seems like common sense, but you'd be surprised how often we do just the opposite.

I went to the beach for fall break. And, as luck would have it, our chairs were next to a group of friends. One girl in the group wore this very flattering white bikini. It was a mom thong, and she was killin' it, folks. She was fit, and tone, and super healthy—with abs and buns of steel. You couldn't hate her because you knew she had worked her butt off for it. But, I immediately thought of my daddy. "Notice what successful people do and do that."

So, I watched her. While her friends were poppin' White Claws, she was drinking water. And, when they passed out snack bags of chips and Cheez-Its, she pulled out a sandwich bag of broccoli. Y'all, that's some serious discipline right there.

I can't tell you how many times I've wanted to lose 20 pounds, buy a new car, or build a new house. But, I can tell you the number of times I've truly sacrificed to make any of that happen.

I'm quite lacking in the motivation and dedication department. I want it handed to me. I don't really wanna work for it. But, you wanna know what I will do? Whine, complain, and compare my situation to others.

What if Noah had done that instead of taking action? Talk about a soggy disaster!

Success is no accident, folks.

Many imagine.

Few execute.

Here's to tackling the day like a boss.

*　　*　　*

> *"Don't let anyone think less of you because you*
> *are young. Be an example to all believers*
> *in what you say, in the way you live, in your love, your*
> *faith, and in your purity." 1 Timothy 4:12*

*　　*　　*

Who is a good example in your life? Why?

_____

_____

_____

_____

_____

_____

_____

What good qualities do they possess?

_____

_____

_____

_____

_____

_____

Where do you need more discipline in your life?

_____

_____

_____

_____

_____

_____

Who do you know that you would consider successful? Why?

_____

_____

_____

_____

_____

_____

How do you think they got there?

_____

_____

_____

_____

_____

_____

Day #4

The Burnt Butt

If you're from the South, it is a sin not to love BBQ and sweet tea. It's also a sin not to participate in local church fundraisers. True story!

So, when a Catholic church in my community was selling Boston butts, I was ready with my wallet. They've done this fundraiser for twelve years, and it's always so yummy. But, not this time... or so they thought.

They used different equipment this year, so the timing was off and all the butts got charred. They were devastated, folks, and attempted to make it right by offering everyone a full refund AND one burnt butt.

I declined the refund, but I gladly accepted that butt. I'm a carnivore and eating meat is what I do—charred or not. So, I told my hubby we would be having BBQ sandwiches and sweet potato fries for dinner. However, once I unwrapped our meat, I wasn't so sure. When they said charred, they weren't kidding.

From the outside, it didn't look too promising. I imagine many folks just chunked it right into the trash. But, as I got to digging, I noticed something miraculous. The inside had been cooked to perfection. It was juicy and yummy and worthy of slathering with a little Sweet Baby Ray's. And that's when I realized, the local Catholic church had taught me a mighty big lesson.

Don't judge a burnt butt by its cover. A poor coat might just hide a rich heart. But, it's bigger than that, folks.

Don't ever give up on someone with a damaged spirit! The world can be a really cruel place. Many people develop a tough skin for survival.

But, once you dig deep and get to know somebody, you'll see their goodness, their worth. And then you can slather them in some Sweet Baby Ray's. Nah. Don't do that. A tough hide usually leads to a tender heart, and I had forgotten that.

The moment you're ready to throw in the towel is usually the moment right before the miracle happens. Don't give up—especially on someone you love OR something you believe in.

*   *   *

"But the Lord told him, "Samuel, don't think he is the one just because he's tall and handsome. He isn't the one I've chosen. People judge others by what they look like, but I judge people by what is in their hearts." 1 Samuel 16:7

*   *   *

Describe a time you have wrongly judged someone.

_____

_____

_____

_____

_____

_____

What did that experience teach you about yourself?

_____

_____

_____

How do you keep it from happening again?

Day #5

Skipping School

We skipped school Friday.

I'm pretty sure it's not an excused absence, but I really don't care. Saturday and Sunday just aren't enough sometimes. Plus, perfect attendance is highly overrated... unless you're into that sorta thing. If workin' for that piece of paper at the end of the school year is important to you, then keep workin' for it. Neither of us is right or wrong. Our priorities are just different.

Mine got rearranged after I blinked and my older children (ages 25 and 29) had left the nest. It was during the painful silence that I realized I had royally screwed the pooch. So many times I should have taken the day off to create memories and savor moments with my babies, but I didn't. It also happened after I resigned from a job of 13 years. It was a job I had POURED my heart and soul into, and all I received at my departure was a thank you and a letter-opener that I threw into the trash. Lesson learned. And then, there's the summer I just knew I was dying. Bad mammogram after bad mammogram and questionable biopsies had me thinking the worst. These three events CHANGED EVERYTHING for me, and I promised myself that I would NEVER forget how they made me feel.

*** In the blink of an eye, everything can change, folks. ***

Life is not a stroll or a journey. It's a freakin' NASCAR race, and it's passing us by at 200 mph. Therefore, we can't waste a minute of it—not a single minute.

So, when I say this baby boy is spoiled, I'm not even kidding. (Note: There's a tremendous difference between being spoiled and being spoiled rotten.) He gets all our time and energy, and I'm pretty proud of how he's turned out. He's smart, like his reading level is way past mine kinda smart. And, he's kind, compassionate, oh so funny, and he has the best manners. So, when his daddy wanted to skip school and take him hunting, this mama said, "What are you waiting for? Go!"

And, it proved to be a fruitful trip. Bo shot his 1st buck sitting in the stand right beside his daddy. Y'all, the hootin' and hollerin' when they found it was PRICELESS! It was pure, unfiltered joy and much like the welcoming I expect to receive when Jesus calls me home. When they discovered the deer just inside the wood line, Bo didn't run straight to the deer. He ran straight to his daddy. And, it was one of those magical Hallmark kinda hugs, where you just can't believe the moment is really happening. Talk about a memory! That's the good stuff, folks.

Life is not a rehearsal. This is it, guys.

Make it count. No (more) regrets!

*   *   *

"I will praise you as long as I live, and in your name I will lift up my hands." Psalm 63:4

*   *   *

What's your event that changed everything for you?

_____

_____

_____

_____

_____

_____

How do you make each day count?

_____

_____

_____

_____

_____

_____

Day #6

Taking Notice

Years ago, when I was still recovering from depression, I read a book. It was called *The Noticer* by Andy Andrews. It's a phenomenal book whose main character is a man named Jones... and I think I met him yesterday. In fact, I know I did.

I recently ordered this book for a good friend, and Amazon delivered it on Thursday. I could not help myself. I re-read the entire book while sitting inside my truck. So, Jones (and his description) are fresh in my mind: older gentleman, leathered skin, longer grey hair, faded jeans, white T-shirt, and sandals. I KNOW it was him, and I'm not surprised.

On my way home from Zumba yesterday morning, while crossing over Hwy. 129, I heard a loud pop. What in the world? It was my back right tire. I had suffered a pretty massive blow out. Fortunately, I was able to pull over at the entrance of a local high school. So, now what? I did what any girl would do. I changed that tire!

(Ha! Absolutely not! I immediately called my hubby to come save me.)

I knew it would be a while before he got there AND it was a gorgeous day, so I proceeded to lower my tailgate and wait in the sunshine. I was a bonafide hood ornament, folks. I bet fifty cars passed by before "Jones" slowly pulled over. And, another fifty cars passed by after he left. He was the one, folks, THE ONLY ONE to stop, so that sorta makes him special.

"Are you okay? I hate to see anybody stuck."

That was it. That was all he said to me because then my mouth took over. I just rambled about anything and everything to him. Craziness! I wish he had been more eloquent with his words, but that would have been out of character. But, now that I think about it, what he said had been enough.

"Are you okay? I hate to see anybody stuck."

Jones, from the novel, was a noticer. He noticed all the things we often overlook. All the big Ds were on his radar: defeat, doubt, despair, discouragement, depression, and even divorce. He would spend the next chapter helping his troubled friend to see the light and they always would. But, what if he hadn't taken the time to notice? What if he hadn't taken the time to pull over and be slightly inconvenienced?

We currently have friends who are stuck in some major ruts...

> Grieving a loss
> Battling depression
> Going through a divorce
> Missing a loved one
> Unhappy in their job
> Doubting their worth
> Losing hope
> Questioning their faith
> Wanting better friends
> Giving up on Mr. Right
> Needing answers
> Waiting on a prayer
> Hoping for a miracle

"Are you okay? I hate to see anybody stuck."

That's all they need to hear from us, folks. It's okay to love them where they're at, but you've also gotta love them enough not to leave them there.

Notice the friends you haven't heard from in awhile. Notice the friends who always text back with: "I'm fine or I'm okay." Because "I'm okay," is never okay. They're currently the ones doggie-paddling the hardest to keep from drowning. Start with them first.

"It is easy to sit up and take notice. What is difficult is getting up and taking action."

*   *   *

"What good is it if someone says he has faith but does not have works? Can that faith save him? Suppose a friend is without clothes and daily food. If you say to them, "Go in peace; keep warm and well fed," but do nothing about their physical needs, what good is it? So you see, faith by itself isn't enough. Unless it produces good deeds, it is dead and useless." James 2:14-17

*   *   *

Describe a time when you felt stuck.

_____

_____

_____

_____

_____

_____

_____

What kept you trapped there?

_____

_____

_____

_____

_____

_____

_____

What have you noticed lately?

_____

_____

_____

_____

_____

_____

_____

Who in your life always takes action?

_____

_____

_____

_____

_____

_____

_____

Hey. Are you okay?

_____

_____

_____

_____

_____

_____

_____

Day #7

Never Swerve

Y'all, my daddy would be so proud of me. He gave me some stellar advice when I was sixteen years old, and it came in handy this morning (at 47 years old).

I ran over a opossum on my way to the gym. It was all his fault for attempting to cross in front of my slightly speeding vehicle. My headlights caused him to freeze. He didn't go left, right, or nothing. He just froze and prepared for impact, but so did I.

My daddy taught me to never—absolutely never—swerve to miss an animal on the road. I'm to grip that wheel at 3 o'clock and 9 o'clock and prepare for impact. At that time, he had witnessed too many people injured (or worse) while trying to avoid an animal. So, I did just that. I clutched the wheel and braced myself. The "impact" was more like a speed bump, but I was safe, my truck was unscathed, and I was alive to share this story. That opossum… not so much.

But, how many times do we "swerve" to avoid a real problem or an issue? Lots! And, how many times does our swerving make matters worse? Tons! Because now we have an issue AND resentment. An issue AND bitterness. An issue AND frustration. You get the idea.

What we need is a friendly officer to pull us over. "M'am, do you realize you were swerving back there?" But, that's what our closest friends will do for us. They are the first ones to notice when we're avoiding a problem. But, here's the thing about that: when we miss the pain, we miss the healing, too.

*   *   *

Check out Isaiah 43:2! "When you pass through the waters, I will be with you; and when you pass through the rivers, they will not sweep over you. When you walk through the fire, you will not be burned; the flames will not set you ablaze."

*   *   *

It never says to swerve around the waters, or the rivers, or the fire. Nope. It says pass THROUGH them. There's a mighty big difference there, folks.

Today's Tip: Sometimes you just gotta hit a problem head on. Jesus, take the wheel!

What problems have you been purposely avoiding?

_____

_____

_____

_____

_____

_____

How do problems we avoid ever get resolved?

_____

_____

_____

_____

_____

When we miss the pain, we miss the healing, too. What needs healing in your life?

_____

_____

_____

_____

_____

_____

_____

Week Three

Sisterhood

"The best kind of friendships are fierce lady friendships where you aggressively believe in each other, defend each other, and think the other deserves the world." Many people call this a tribe, but when you are soul sisters, there's only one thing it can be. Ain't no hood like sisterhood!

> *Dear Lord, you have blessed me with true friends. Comfort them in their times of strife. Bless them with good health and happiness. Keep them safe and secure. Surround them with love, laughter, and plenty of patience when dealing with me. In Jesus's name, Amen.*

Week Three

PRAYER JOURNAL

Who will you pray for this week? What situations need God's guidance? Where does Jesus need to intervene? How can the Holy Spirit help? Date it and state it! Pray for these things each day this week. Update it as needed.

Day #1

Walk Away

My mama always told me, "You're gonna become like who you hang around." I thought that was so dumb at thirteen years old. At forty-seven, not so much. Every small step in the right direction counts, folks.

There will be people who tell you you're wasting your time. **Walk away**.

There will be people who won't see your worth. **Walk away**.

There will be people who won't understand your passion. **Walk away**.

There will be people whose actions don't match their words. **Walk away**.

There will be people who document your every fault when you overlook all of theirs. **Walk away**.

There will be people you can never please. **Walk away**.

There will be people who always throw stones. **Walk away**.

There will be people who threaten your peace, self respect, and morals. **Walk away**.

There will be people who gossip, create drama, and stir the pot. **Don't walk away. Run**!

But, there will also be people who see your worth. **Walk towards them**.

There will be people who support your passion. **Walk towards them**.

There will be people who are filled with love and grace. **Walk towards them**.

There will be people who know your heart and your intentions. **Walk towards them**.

There will be people who believe in you more than you believe in yourself. **Walk towards them**.

There will be people who drop everything to help fill a void. **Walk towards them**.

There will be people filled with genuine encouragement, positive enthusiasm, and contagious laughter. **Walk towards them**.

There will be people who make your day brighter just by being in it. **Walk towards them**.

There will be people so loyal and honest that you never have to question their friendship. **Run like hell towards them**.

*   *   *

"People with integrity walk safely, but those who follow crooked paths will be exposed." Proverbs 10:9

*   *   *

You can't fully let go without first walking away. What or who do you need to walk away from?

_____

_____

_____

_____

_____

_____

Who makes you wanna lace up your sneakers and run as fast as you can towards them? Why?

_____

_____

_____

_____

_____

_____

Day #2

Don't Dim Your Light

Life Tip #1: Let go of the crap that suffocates your soul!

For me, that's the irrelevant opinions of others, and letting that mess go has been a game changer. I didn't get here overnight though. I used to worry myself sick over what people were thinking, did they like me, would I be included, would I even fit in. But, my days of chasing people are O-V-E-R!

Once upon a time, I actually dimmed my light because it was too bright for some people. What a hot mess AND what a slap in the face to God! He gave me that light, folks. And, He gave you yours, too. [Note: If you have to tiptoe around others, you're not walking with your tribe.] And, when you start to see your worth, you'll find it harder and harder to spend time with people who don't.

So, I prefer to stay close to the people who make me feel like sunshine—the light bringers, the magic makers, and the game changers. These people don't let me play small with my life. They challenge me and uplift me. They hold me accountable. These heartbeats are my people… and I need them like oxygen and water.

Jesus healed a paralyzed man because of the faith of that man's friends. So, don't think who you spend your time with is not important. It's everything!

* * *

"As iron sharpens iron, so a friend sharpens a friend." Proverbs 27:17

* * *

Whose opinion do you need to silence? Why?

_____

_____

_____

_____

_____

_____

_____

Who is in your tribe? What blessings do they bring to your life?

_____

_____

_____

_____

_____

_____

PS: You should probably tell them. :-)

Day #3

When You Know Better, Do Better

When my baby boy and I were on our 30 day road trip, our goal was to drive four hours each day, pitch our tent, do a little sightseeing, and then move along the next morning to our next location.

Well, yesterday went as smoothly as could be. We even hiked to the bottom of a huge waterfall. It was getting back up (to the parking lot) that was the challenge. As our reward, we treated ourselves to junk food AND an ice cream from the campground snack bar. It was there that Bo spotted him.

He was an elderly man surrounded by his family. They were all waiting on their burgers and fries. But, Bo was shocked that the gentleman smoked a cigarette while he waited. I tried to assure Bo that it was fine because he was outdoors. That's when I got the, "OMG, mom! Look at him."

Yep, he had all kinds of breathing tubes and tanks and hoses attached to him... yet he was still chain smoking while waiting on his meal. What kinda self-sabotage is that?!? But, guys, we're all guilty of that kinda behavior.

I've noticed my body doesn't really like dairy—cheese, sour cream, milkshakes from Chick-Fil-A. But, I still ate my whole pizza... and felt miserable afterwards. Ugh. I knew better.

I have a friend on the verge of diabetes, but she keeps eating all the most sugary things. Why?

Another friend takes meds for high blood pressure, but she's still eating tons (and I do mean tons) of red meat. She hasn't cut back even a little bit. Why?

But, that self-sabotaging behavior affects more than our health.

A friend got passed over for a promotion, but she's always late to work.

A friend hates how cluttered her house is, but she never takes time to clean it—like never.

A friend is struggling financially, yet she keeps using multiple credit cards.

Heck. I used to hang around the wrong crowd. I wanted to fit in. I wanted them to like me. But, they weren't right for me. It was like trying to fit a square peg in a round hole. They did not push me to be my best. They were happy with mediocre. Fortunately, I broke those chains, but continuing crazy friendships is a form of self-sabotage.

Last example, it's pretty clear the life we're supposed to be living. The Bible is filled with detailed instructions and parables. Every Sunday pulpits across the nation are filled with passionate preachers trying to guide us to salvation. Yet, some of us continue to miss the mark. The devil doesn't have to tempt us because we're screwing up our everlasting life ourselves.

Today's lesson: when you know better, do better. Period.

*   *   *

*"But small is the gate and narrow the road that leads
to life, and only a few find it." Matthew 7:14*

*   *   *

What self-sabotaging behaviors do you have?

_____

_____

_____

_____

_____

_____

How can a good group of friends help you with these behaviors?

_____

_____

_____

_____

_____

_____

How can you and Jesus tackle these behaviors?

_____

_____

_____

_____

_____

_____

Day #4

But... Not Today

So, there's currently a hawk in my backyard. He's sitting on one of our swings by the pool. I'm pretty sure he's looking for breakfast. We currently have tons of nests and baby birds around our house. It's like a breakfast buffet. But... not today.

This hawk could single handedly eat each individual parent. ALONE—they're pretty defenseless against his razor sharp talons and beak. But, TOGETHER—they're a force to reckon with, folks. They all swarmed that hawk this morning. Maybe he just wasn't feelin' it. Maybe it was too much work. Maybe he knew where to find an easier meal. Regardless, he bowed out and left the scene without his breakfast. Their babies were saved.

In my mind, the devil kinda works this same way. He sits, patiently and confidently, searching for the easiest prey. He's ready to swoop down at any moment and grab hold of our thoughts. Instead of talons, he uses doubt, discouragement, anger, bitterness, and jealousy. This is why attending church is so important. This is why having a tribe is so important. This is why joining a small group is so important. This is why reading your Bible is so important. ALONE—we are defenseless against his antics. But, TOGETHER—he doesn't stand a chance. Your church will pray for you. Your friends will help you. Matthew, Mark, Luke, and John will guide you, and Jesus will save you.

The devil will try to distract us and distance us. But... not today!

Alone... we are strong.

Together... we are stronger.

Amy Bowdoin

*   *   *

*"Two people are better off than one, for they can
help each other succeed." Ecclesiastes 4:9*

*   *   *

Describe a time when you tried to go it all alone.

_____

_____

_____

_____

_____

_____

Describe a time you joined a group and were victorious.

_____

_____

_____

_____

_____

_____

Why is a tribe of friends so important to have?

_____

_____

_____

_____

_____

_____

_____

Day #5

Hold My Earrings

So, I recently shared how someone unfollowed me on Facebook. It must have been a battle cry because that post rallied the troops. It got more hits, likes, shares, and comments than ever before, like record-breaking comments. And, I read every single one of them.

Some were from dear friends who have known me my whole life and still claim me. Others were from people who know me now (after I've rebounded from rock bottom). A few were from my ride or die tribe. I'd expect nothing less from them. A couple were from acquaintances I haven't heard from in decades. I didn't even know they read these posts. But, the majority of comments came from "friends" I've picked up along the way. At some point, you read something that resonated with you, so you've stuck around. And, I greatly appreciate your support.

But, regardless of the connection, your words of encouragement and affirmation were just what this Georgia peach needed. But, it was more than your words. It was your actions. You put love in motion when you stopped what you were doing to pour into me. The world kinda needs more of that, folks.

In my tribe, we have a saying. "Hold my earrings." That means…

> It's about to go down.
> I'm here for you.
> I'm willing to fight.
> You are not alone.
> I've got your back.
> Relax. We've got this.

And, I feel like you said all that to me last week. But, I also got to witness it again this past weekend. We were on a girls' trip—also known as Moms Gone Wild. It was late and we may or may not have been a bit rowdy and filled with spirits. We were laughing and dancing around the campfire to a little Maroon 5. It was good old-fashioned girl time. And then our neighbors walked up. Hmmmm... That doesn't sound sketchy at all, but it's midnight and my mama always said, "Nothin' good happens after midnight."

The entire exchange was awkward. And, I'm definitely leaving out some details. Let's just say, "That escalated quickly." and one of my friends became very uncomfortable. But, no worries! Once another friend realized this she immediately said, "Hold my earrings." And, that heifer single handedly shut them down—all five of them. She sent them packing with a quickness all because she saw a friend in need. She didn't wait. She didn't think about it. She didn't need to talk it over. Nope. She saw a friend in distress, so she pounced like a spider monkey. The world kinda needs more of that, too.

So, today's lesson is an easy one: Be that friend, guys. Be the one who says, "Hold my earrings." and pounces into action. That kinda love is needed far more than you know.

*   *   *

*"A friend loves at all times, and a brother is born
for a time of adversity." Proverbs 17:17*

*   *   *

Who would you say, "Hold my earrings" for?

_____

_____

_____

_____

_____

_____

Describe a time you jumped into action for a friend.

_____

_____

_____

_____

_____

_____

How can you be a better friend today?

_____

_____

_____

_____

_____

_____

Day #6

Girlfriend Code #1

[Warning: There's an ugly word in today's post, but I'm trying to keep it PG by camouflaging it with dollar signs. I'm also trying to keep it real. I can't change what was actually said in that heated moment, or this would be fake news… and that stuff is already everywhere.]

So, I've got this friend. I'm gonna call her "Queenie" because that's her extremely fitting nickname.

Well, Queenie was one of my very first friends when I started a new job. And, when I say friend, I mean it. None of that back-stabbing acquaintance kinda stuff. She was genuine and authentic.

She was also loyal, and passionate, and fierce in her convictions. And, we quickly became thick as thieves (Real people have a way of finding each other, folks). We exercised together. We vacationed together. She was the only one I allowed to keep my baby. Yep, from birth to elementary school, I trusted only her with my child. True story!

For the sake of transparency, I'm sharing our age difference. She's a little older than me—by almost 10 years (and now she's gonna slice my tires). But, that also makes her wise, folks, and everyone needs a wise friend. She's been there. She's seen it, done it, read about it, talked about it, researched it, you name it. So, she is always teaching me things. And, I'll NEVER forget the day she taught me "Girlfriend Code #1."

This one lady at work kinda rubbed her the wrong way. She was always doing petty things. Well, one day Queenie was carrying a ton of books and that lady would not open the door for her. Rude, right?!? So, by the time she made it to my classroom, she was fired up, folks. In my foolishness, I attempted to calm the situation by playing devil's advocate. "Maybe she didn't see you? Maybe she was just having a bad day? Maybe her arms were weighed down, too?"

Well, Queenie did not like my response (and this is when I got schooled, folks). She slammed every book she had been holding on my desk like a dad-gum thunderbolt. She then came across the table and pointed her finger in my face while she said...

"When I tell you she did me wrong, you don't justify it. All you say is, 'I can't believe she would do that to you. Let's go kick her a$$.' THAT is Girlfriend Code #1."

Guys, I have NEVER forgotten that lesson. When one of my friends has an issue with someone else, I'm there. I don't even ask questions. So long, devil's advocate. So long, trying to justify rude behavior. "Hold my earrings!" is all that matters.

That is code for...

> I'm willing to fight.
> I've got your back.
> You are worth it.
> I am here.
> I don't care what the world is saying. I believe you!
> You are not alone.
> I'm done with that crazy heifer.
> When a red flag goes up for you, it goes up for the both of us. Truth!
> I'm bringing over the Margaritas and chocolate.
> Nothing else matters.
> You don't have to doubt or worry.
> You are right.
> You're looking good. Have you lost 10 pounds?
> A friend loves at all times—even the yucky ones.
> Stay seated. I've got this one!

That is code—the Girlfriend Code—and it is one of God's greatest blessings!

*   *   *

"A sweet friendship refreshes the soul." Proverbs 27:9

*   *   *

How do you fight for your friends?

_____

_____

_____

_____

_____

_____

_____

Explain a time when you used the Girlfriend Code to help a friend.

_____

_____

_____

_____

_____

_____

_____

Describe a time a friend fought for YOU.

_____

_____

_____

_____

_____

_____

_____

Day #7

Keep Your Circle Small

Once upon a time, I had this unfounded idea that everyone needed to be my friend. The good. The bad. The ugly. The sinners, and the saints. You get the idea.

My genuine love for others had me socializing with anyone and everyone, but something wasn't quite right. They shared my interests, but they didn't all share my values. What would Jesus do? Oh, He'd be right there with me. He purposefully sought out the crippled, the unworthy, and the morally wrong. But, it's taken me A LONG TIME to realize He didn't invite them to His table.

The Last Supper: If there was ever a time to have a farewell throwdown and invite the whole neighborhood, this was it. But, Jesus didn't. He saved that moment for only His friends—his true friends. It was small. It was intimate. And, that's what made it meaningful.

I could have spared myself a lot of heartache had I known the difference between an acquaintance and a true friend. A true friend is a gift from God. They encourage you. They strengthen you, and they make you better. But, an acquaintance? Those jokers are a dime a dozen, and the devil had me believing that I needed them. What a devious distraction!

The wrong crowd delayed my purpose. Oh, but the right crowd... those beautiful, strong women fanned my flames and pushed me towards my calling.

So, here's today's takeaway:

We can be friendly (and compassionate, and encouraging, and kind) without being "friends." Keep your circle small. Jesus did.

* * *

"The righteous choose their friends carefully, but the way of the wicked leads them astray." Proverbs 12:26

* * *

Describe a time you were surrounded by the wrong friends.

_____
_____
_____
_____
_____
_____
_____

How did you know it wasn't a good fit for you?

_____
_____
_____
_____
_____
_____
_____

What are the benefits from keeping your circle small?

_____

_____

_____

_____

_____

_____

_____

Proverbs 12:26 states to choose your friends carefully. How do you do that?

_____

_____

_____

_____

_____

_____

_____

Week Four

Fresh Air

I'm a mom of all boys, and they have one thing in common: the need to pass gas while I'm trapped inside the car with them. It's awful, folks. But, as soon as this happens, I quickly roll down every window in my vehicle and breathe in the fresh air. And, at that moment, it's so darn refreshing that I kinda know I need more of it. "A breath of fresh air is a great thing to take—and an even better thing to be."

> *Dear Lord, breathe life into my discouraged spirit. Replenish my energy and revive my heart, so that I can be a blessing to those around me. Help me to soak up your word and your promises in order to be a breath of fresh air to others. In Jesus's name, Amen.*

PRAYER JOURNAL

*Who will you pray for this week? What situations need
God's guidance? Where does Jesus need to intervene? How
can the Holy Spirit help? Date it and state it! Pray for
these things each day this week. Update it as needed.*

Day #1

From the Inside Out

I've noticed, as I've gotten older and my backside has gotten wider, that my hair has gotten thinner—like much thinner.

I'm working out twice a day to reach my goal weight, and my hair follicles are the only thing getting results. The rest of me is stuck-like-Chuck and not budging. But, ain't that how it usually goes?!?

So now, I'm researching hair products like there's no tomorrow. I'm not opposed to pills, lotions, ointments, gels, spells, or voodoo rituals. I just need my hair to get thicker—like much thicker.

So, I took my daddy's sage advice and asked a friend for guidance. But, this is not just any friend. It's my friend with the most beautiful hair, so thick and glamorous with absolutely every strand in place. If anyone would know how to help me, she would.

> What did she tell me to do?
> "Take Biotin."
> "Like the vitamin? Or in a shampoo?"
> "Most definitely the vitamin!"
> "Why?
> (And, here's where I need you paying attention.)
> "Because we heal from the inside out."
> Let that line sink in a minute, folks.

How many times have I avoided a difficult conversation out of fear? Several!

How many times have I harbored bitterness instead of dealing with the issue? Lots!

How many times have I intentionally kept the drama alive? Too many to count!

How many times have I attempted to ignore a problem (allowing it to eat away at me) without voicing my concern? A ridiculous amount!

How many times have I beat myself up over something I can't change? It's infinite!

And, guess what? No amounts of "I'm sorry" from others is gonna fix it.

Until I address MY heart, nothing is changing, folks. Not even a little bit. The healing has to start with me—from the inside out!

So, what's today's lesson? Don't become a hostage to bitterness, anger, resentment, or past mistakes. Forgive yourself first.

*   *   *

"Indeed, the very hairs of your head are all numbered. Don't be afraid; you are worth more than many sparrows." Luke 12:7

*   *   *

What's been holding you hostage from the inside?

_____

_____

_____

_____

_____

_____

_____

What will it take for you to forgive yourself? What will it take to forget?

_____

_____

_____

_____

_____

_____

_____

Day #2

Set Apart

You are special.

At some point in your life a parent, grandparent, spouse, teacher or friend told you that.

And, you believed it.

So, what happened?

I already know the answer because I've been there. You fell for the devil's trap. There's no need for shame or guilt because we've ALL been there!

I blame it on awareness.

I was pretty proud of my B, until I saw she had made an A.

I was thrilled with my 3rd place ribbon, until I saw she had won a trophy.

I liked my black car, until I saw she had bought a new white one.

I was happy with my tent, until I saw she had purchased a camper.

I was excited to lose 10 pounds, until I saw she had lost 15. That heifer!

I was content with my marriage, my job, my children, my life... until I saw hers.

Oh, sweet comparison, you ruin everything!

I'll be 47 years old in a few months, and I bet I've spent over half my life feeling inadequate. That's 23 YEARS of feeling like I'm not enough. That is insane, folks. Now add to that an over-the-top need to follow the crowd and a psycho desire to fit in, and you've got the recipe for a disaster.

Why would I feel special when I'm always coming up short? Why would I feel special when I'm clearly not enough?

Such classic questions asked by someone who has totally forgotten her worth. So, let me remind you.

YOU are the daughter of the one true king, and He sacrificed His only son just for you—so that you might live a prosperous life. You can't do that when you're busy counting the blessings of others while constantly overlooking your own. (Read that last line again, folks.)

I don't know about you, but I don't keep my fancy china anywhere near my everyday dishes or paper plates. I set my special ones apart... just like God did with you.

*   *   *

{Before I formed you in your mother's womb, I knew you... AND I SET YOU APART. Jeremiah 1:5}

*   *   *

He set you apart on purpose! No wonder you struggle with fitting in. You were never meant to blend in. You were born to stand out... but you can't do that when you're lost in the crowd. (Warning: You've gotta be extra careful when you follow the masses because sometimes that "m" is silent.)

But, there's an even bigger reason for avoiding the crowds. "The Bible is not filled as much with mass movements as it is with individuals who were willing to stand alone."

Describe a time you fell for the comparison trap.

_____

_____

_____

_____

_____

_____

_____

How are you willing to set yourself apart?

_____

_____

_____

_____

_____

_____

_____

Today's goal: Don't let comparison dull your sparkle. Choose to shine!

Day #3

Something in the Water

When we were on our cross-country road trip, sometimes we had service. Sometimes we didn't. That was the case at Glacier National Park. Fortunately, my camera always works. I want you to look very carefully at these two photos. Zoom in if you must. Pay close attention to the rocks.

The rocks on the shore are all dried up—almost grey looking. But, the rocks in the water are incredible—so bright and so colorful. And, the way the sun hits the water almost makes them shine. But, the funny thing is… they're all the same rocks. When I'd take a dry rock and place it in the water, it would be just as pretty as the rest of them. But, when I'd take a rock from the water and place it on the shore, it would morph into an old grey rock just like all the rest. There must be something in the water, huh?

So, I bottled it up and will be selling 8 ounces for $10 when I return home. Bwaa Haa Haa! But, there really is a deeper meaning here.

You can play it safe on the sidelines—or on the shore. But, you'll never reach your full potential that way. You've gotta jump in the water. Oh, yes. You might get tossed about, but that's how God smooths our edges, folks.

So, if you're tired of feeling exhausted, frustrated, or "all dried up," I've got the answer. All you need is some living water and a little bit of "son" shine.

*   *   *

*On the last and greatest day of the festival,
Jesus stood and said in a loud voice,
"Let anyone who is thirsty come to me and
drink. Whoever believes in me,
as the scripture has said, "Out of his heart will
flow rivers of living water." John 7:37-38*

*   *   *

What has you feeling exhausted?

_____

_____

_____

_____

_____

_____

_____

In which areas of your life do you always play it safe?

_____

_____

_____

_____

_____

_____

_____

Why is soaking up the "son" shine so important in your walk with Jesus?

Day #4

Ready to Pounce

My hubby was out of town on a hunting trip, leaving me home alone with my baby boy. Well, something scared him making the thought of me leaving him at 5 AM for the gym too much to bear. He would have been asleep the whole time I was gone, but the thought of being alone was too much. So, I opted to stay home and try the Couch to 5K app in my driveway. Something beats nothing, right?

Well, about halfway through my workout, a Chevy truck with a pretty impressive lift kit came creeping by my house. It slowly pulled into the neighborhood across the street. No worries! We all slow down before a turn. But, within a few minutes, it was back at the entrance, just sitting there… watching me. Stalking me!

I'm pretty sure they were fiddle-farting with their cell phones and a slightly overweight, middle-aged woman was not a top priority, but my son had planted a seed. Something was out to get us, so naturally my mind wandered to season 3, episode 12 of "Criminal Minds." Old Chevy truck, lift kit, tinted windows… the only thing missing was some over-the-top heavy metal music blaring from the windows. So, at this point, I'm convinced the driver is a trained sniper and I'm his next target. I could feel my heart rate start to rise. I spooked myself, folks.

At that very moment, my dog Knox stepped out of the garage. He was angled straight at that truck. He was standing there, so strong, so able, and ready to pounce. He's not barking. There's no need. In the glare of the floodlights, he looked like a mighty lion. Just his presence calmed my fears. Within seconds, the truck turned and never returned, and my dog slowly resumed his sleeping position in the garage. Crisis averted.

I couldn't help but think, that right there is what it's like to put on the armor of God. When we need him most is when he steps in between us and the enemy. He's there, so strong, so able, and ready to pounce. Just His presence calms our fears. How great is our God!

*   *   *

"You put a wall of protection around him and his home and his property. You have made him prosper in everything he does." Job 1:10

*   *   *

When might you need the armor of God?

_____

_____

_____

_____

_____

_____

Why would you need a "wall of protection" around your thoughts?

_____

_____

_____

_____

_____

_____

Our thoughts are mighty powerful. What truths do you speak to yourself?

_____

_____

_____

_____

_____

_____

_____

Day #5

Withstanding the Storm

We've all heard Forrest Gump's famous line, "Life is like a box of chocolates. You never know what you're gonna get." But, guys, it's chocolate. Either way you're winning. What about rotten tomatoes? How well do you handle those?

As much as I'd love for my child's life to be rainbows, and sunshine, and chocolate, that's just not how the world works. I'd be doing him a tremendous disservice if I constantly sheltered him from rotten tomatoes. He needs those yucky experiences just as much—if not more—than all the yummy ones.

We recently went tent camping, just the two of us. The day called for 80% rain. I thought about canceling, but where's the lesson in that? I can't have him thinking life is always blue skies and smooth sailing. He needs to know storms are part of life, too, and how he handles those storms will determine the quality of his life.

So, it rained… for forty days and nights. Ha. Just kidding, but it did rain. There was crazy thunder and lightning, too. We could see it coming across the lake.

"What should we do?"

I asked him that question, and I took his lead (Note: Children need to learn problem solving skills, too). He put our chairs in my truck, so they'd be dry after the storm passed. Smart guy! He also grabbed a cold water and some snacks before we hunkered down in our tent.

"Now what, buddy?"

That's when he pulled out a board game from our suitcase. Perfect! We snacked. We talked. We laughed. We played a very intense game of Animalopoly. It's kinda like Monopoly but way more fun. Before we knew it, the storm had passed and we were back to blue skies and smooth sailing.

> "I'm glad that's over."
> "Me, too."
> "But, it wasn't that bad."
> "You wanna know why?"
> "Why, mom?"
> "Because you didn't give the storm any power. Remember that."

I could tell he was deep in thought and stewing on my words as he retrieved our dry chairs from my truck. Lesson learned.

*   *   *

"He calmed the storm to a whisper; the waves of the sea were hushed."
Psalm 107:29

*   *   *

What storms in your life are you feeding?

_____

_____

_____

_____

_____

_____

What can you do to withstand the storm? What changes must you be willing to make?

_____

_____

_____

_____

_____

_____

_____

Day #6

Making Room

I'm super embarrassed to admit this, but I just recently got my life back in order. Apparently, it's been spiraling outta control since May of 2012. That was the date on the unopened bottle of Hershey's chocolate syrup that was in my pantry. We moved into our current house in 2016, so I packed and relocated an already old bottle of syrup. Lord, what was I thinking?

Our pantry was crammed to the max, which prompted "The Great Closet Clean-out." But, now I know why. Everything was outta date. Apparently, when it comes to food, this heifer right here is keeping it forever. I even had a box of powdered milk that my mom gave me when she was worried there might be a blizzard. When was the last time we even had a threat of snow?

I threw out five garbage bags full of old food. People actually have more snacks in their desk drawer than we've got food in our pantry right now. It did make grocery shopping a lot easier this weekend. We needed one of everything. Ha! But, it feels good to be organized and up-to-date. It feels refreshing in a weird, why would a clean pantry matter sorta way. And, that got me thinking.

Letting go is the hard part, isn't it?

Chocolate, carbs, anger, bitterness, jealousy, hurt! Even when we know it's no longer good for us, we don't wanna give it up. And that's when I noticed my heart is like my pantry—crammed full of old crap—crammed full of things that weigh me down—crammed full of things that keep me from being who God created me to be. Letting go might be hard, but holding on is harder.

"The first step to getting what you want is having the courage to get rid of what you don't." We gotta make room for our blessings, folks.

* * *

"Dear brothers and sisters, I have not achieved
it, but I focus on this one thing:
Forgetting the past and looking forward to
what lies ahead." Philippians 3:13

* * *

What needs cleaning at your house?

_____

_____

_____

_____

_____

_____

What needs cleaning in your heart?

_____

_____

_____

_____

_____

_____

How might holding on be harder than letting go?

_____

_____

_____

_____

_____

_____

_____

What burdens are you holding on to?

_____

_____

_____

_____

_____

_____

_____

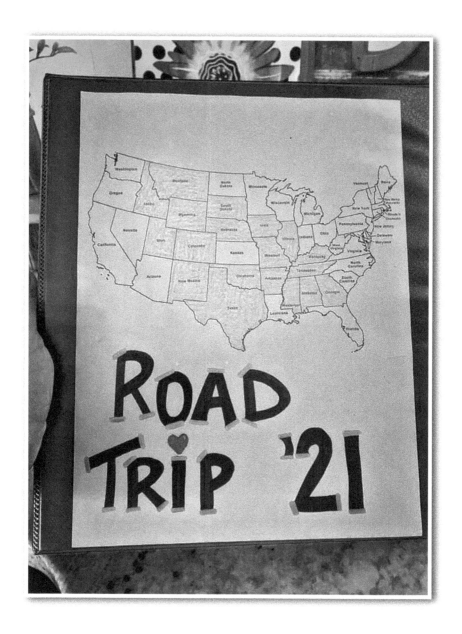

Day #7

Praise the Process

I'm a middle school teacher. I think I've been one for 25 years. It all kinda runs together at this point. I'm sure I'll start counting more precisely the closer I get to thirty.

During this time, I've read hundreds of I.E.P.s. For those of you not familiar with the lingo, that stands for Individualized Educational Plan. Every child should have one, but only the special ones do. In layman's terms, it levels the playing field. It helps them keep up with their peers… kinda like when my ten year old gives me a 30-second head start in a foot race. We can both run. I just need a little leverage to make it fair.

Well, yesterday I was reading an I.E.P. and I noticed something I had previously overlooked. It was so profound I had to read it three times. It's something that good teachers do without thinking, but it's something busy, stressed, overworked, and under-appreciated teachers often forget. And, I really hope you're sitting down, so you can soak it in, too.

** "Praise the process and not just the final product." **

That might be my new favorite line. You may even see me wearing it on a t-shirt in the near future. "Praise the process!" That is golden, folks.

I'm currently raising my third baby boy. I rushed those first two along like it was an Olympic race. I was so consumed with the "final product" that I almost missed the entire race. Some of you are doing this right now with your own babies… always rushing from one thing to another. Stop it! Oh, yes! The days are long, but you're gonna miss the hell outta them. Apply the brakes and praise the process!

I'm also currently training for the trip of a lifetime. I need to be healthy and physically fit to make it happen. But, passing on the dessert sucks. Working out each day sucks. But, guys, that's the attitude of someone consumed with the final product. I'm getting stronger. I can feel it in my lungs. The transformation is happening. I need to praise the process.

But, we're all guilty of focusing on the final product... a wedding, a family, a new house, a promotion, a trip, a new car, good health, graduation, healing, time off, a miracle, friendships, perfecting a craft, recognition, forgiveness, etc... This list could go on and on. And, while the final product is nice, the process is where the magic happens. Think about it, folks. We marvel at the butterfly and seldom praise the caterpillar.

But, it's not always rainbows and butterflies. Sometimes the process is scary. Sometimes the process is hard. And, sometimes it hurts like hell. But God is ALWAYS with us—on the mountaintops, in the valleys, and in our classrooms—shaping, pressing, grooming, molding, teaching, coaching, encouraging, and loving us to completion.

Today's lesson: Praise the process.

*   *   *

"And I am sure of this, that He who began a good work in you will bring it to completion at the day of Jesus Christ." Philippians 1:6

*   *   *

It's refreshing to know we're all works in progress. What are you working on?

_____

_____

_____

_____

_____

_____

_____

What can you praise about your process?

_____

_____

_____

_____

_____

_____

What are you learning along the way?

_____

_____

_____

_____

_____

_____

Week Five

Detours

I'm an over-the-top planner to a fault. My OCD and controlling personality can't handle kinks in my plan. It typically sends me spiraling outta control, and I end up taking my frustrations out on my family. As I've gotten older, I have learned to appreciate the unexpected detours along the way. Why? There's mighty lessons to be learned on roads that are less traveled. Lessons sent by God himself. I hope you're ready to veer.

> *Dear Lord, help me to embrace things that are out of my control. Help me to learn from every detour, road block, and set back. Only you can see the big picture. Fill me with assurance that every bend in the road is a blessing for you. In Jesus's name, Amen.*

PRAYER JOURNAL

Who will you pray for this week? What situations need God's guidance? Where does Jesus need to intervene? How can the Holy Spirit help? Date it and state it! Pray for these things each day this week. Update it as needed.

_____

_____

_____

_____

_____

_____

_____

_____

_____

_____

_____

_____

_____

_____

_____

_____

_____

_____

_____

_____

_____

_____

Day #1

The Power of God's Promises

You're not the same individual you were a year ago or even a few months ago. Life has dealt you some ups and downs. You've learned lessons, solved problems, and burned a few bridges, yet somehow you're still here—still smiling, still waking up to face the same giants that left you restless the night before. That's faith, guys.

No one is immune from sucky situations, sucky people, or sucky days. It's all drama and a headache, but you push through again and again and again. That's faith, too, folks.

The Bible never stated that life would be easy or fair. It never stated our life would be free of difficult people. It never stated we would always have favor and live the sweet life. There's ALWAYS gonna be detours, roadblocks, major delays, and someone just waiting to pull us over and give us grief. Our faith provides us with the strength we need to persevere during these hard times. There's a purpose to this season, so DON'T STOP BELIEVING! (That sounds like some catchy song lyrics to me. Ha.)

"You cannot worship the power of your circumstances AND the power of God's promises at the same time." (Woah! Some of you need to read that line again.)

Feed your faith until your doubts starve to death. How do you do that? You hang around the right people, you read and watch the right things, and you open your heart and invite God into every situation. But, be warned! When God steps in, miracles happen.

Amy Bowdoin

* * *

*"I will repay you for the years the locusts have eaten... Once
again you will have all the food you want, and you will
praise the Lord your God, who does these miracles for you.
Never again will my people be disgraced." Joel 2:25-26*

* * *

How have you changed this year?

_____

_____

_____

_____

_____

_____

_____

What changes still need to be made for you to fulfill God's promises
for your life?

_____

_____

_____

_____

_____

_____

_____

What are some roadblocks you're currently facing?

_____

_____

_____

_____

_____

_____

_____

What could be the "purpose for this season?"

_____

_____

_____

_____

_____

_____

_____

Day #2

His Last Time

Say, "Cheese!"

For those who know me, this next statement is absolute truth.

I am a picture takin' fool.

Why?

"Because you'll never know the true value of a moment until it becomes a memory." That's why. Plus, it's worth a thousand words, right? It tells a story—your story—and I happen to love stories.

So, I went to the beach with my family over the weekend- all of them. My oldest even flew in from Philadelphia to make it happen. Therefore, on our last day, we decided to "close it down," which means we were out there until after sunset. But, God had us right where we needed to be. It's kinda wild how that always happens.

A family was walking the beach, all wearing coordinating colors. So, you know what's up. It's picture taking time. My favorite! Unfortunately, they kept having to rotate being the photographer.

"Jake, go help them. It's the grandfather's last time at the beach."

Naturally, my crew looked at me like I was crazy, but I could just feel it in my gut. So, like a good middle child, he went to assist.

I did get the church giggles because this was not a one-and-done pic. Oh, no! He became the photographer for their full-fledged photo shoot. He took pics of them standing, sitting, hugging, holding hands, and walking into the sunset.

It was 15 minutes before Jake returned to our beach chairs. It was another 15 minutes before the daughter walked up to us. She simply said, "Thank you." With tears in her eyes, she shared, "It's his last time."

This was NOT one of those "I told you so" moments. It was one of those breathe it in and soak it up kinda moments. One of those moments that sticks with you for a while.

Guys, "the last time" is coming for every single one of us.

Take the picture	Make the time	Eat the cake
Take the trip	Laugh until your belly hurts	Watch a sunrise
Savor a sunset	Forgive	Forgive again
Love your people BIG.	Dance like no one's watching.	Buy the dress

But, most importantly, give your heart to Jesus. Goodbyes are only temporary when you know Jesus.

*   *   *

"For God so loved the world that he gave his one and only Son, that whoever believes in him shall not perish but have eternal life." John 3:16

*   *   *

Have you experienced a "last time" with a loved one? How did it change you?

_____

_____

_____

_____

_____

_____

_____

If you could go back in time, what would you do differently?

_____

_____

_____

_____

_____

_____

If tomorrow never comes, how would you spend TODAY?

_____

_____

_____

_____

_____

_____

Day #3

The Panic Button

We recently took our baby boy to TopGolf for his birthday. And, we had a crazy good time. Because we were running late, I drove us there. "Super Speeder" should really be my middle name. But, because I drove us there, my hubby drove us home. We like to trade off duties like that.

Well, I decided to recline my seat and rest my eyes while he decided to call a friend. That was our first mistake, folks. I eventually looked up and asked, "Where are we?" My hubby didn't know either until we spotted a sign. He had missed our exit running that lip. We were now almost 10 miles off course. In classic male fashion, he tried to correct this minor infraction by turning lemons into lemonade.

"We can (now) swing by the grocery and then head home. No biggie."

In classic female fashion, I had to act overly disgruntled by this new inconvenience. So, like a mature woman, I opted to pout and remain in the car while he shopped. But, I kinda think I was right where God needed me to be.

While waiting, I noticed this woman canvassing the parking lot. She carried a fresh bouquet of flowers and one grocery bag. She clearly could not find her car... anywhere. I got the church giggles picturing melting ice cream all in her grocery bag. I know. I know. I'm a horrible person, so I asked the Lord for forgiveness and hoped it was soup, soup that'd be hot and ready to eat when she got home. But, guys, after a while, she did start to panic. Just where was her car?!?

Finally, she asked a nearby employee for help. Clearly, it was an employee who had dealt with this kinda thing before. What was his advice? Hit the panic button. And, that's exactly what she did. In a matter of seconds, her horn was honking, lights flashing, the works. Her car was just one row over. She was so relieved and appreciative. She immediately jumped in her car and was on her way. What a great lesson for me to witness!

She was lost, folks. But, sometimes I lose my way, too. And, just like her, I frantically search in all the wrong places—leaving my Bible as a last resort. I also try to handle it all on my own, which only prolongs my torture. It's very hard for me to hit that panic button, but sometimes it's more than needed—it's required. Sometimes asking for help is the bravest move we can make. It's not weak; it's wise. Remember that, folks.

*   *   *

"If any of you lacks wisdom, you should ASK God, who gives generously to all without finding fault, and it will be given to you. But, when you ASK, you must believe and not doubt, because the one who doubts is like a wave of the sea, blown and tossed by the wind." John 1:5-6

*   *   *

Describe a time when you were "lost."

_____

_____

_____

_____

_____

_____

Who did you ask for help?

_____

_____

_____

_____

_____

_____

_____

Why is asking for help so hard to do?

_____

_____

_____

_____

_____

_____

Who is someone you could help this week?

_____

_____

_____

_____

_____

_____

Day #4

A Cup of Kindness

Have you ever experienced something so inspiring that it left you speechless... for over a month? Well, that recently happened to me. It was January 18th, and I was camping. Imagine that! And while this post has absolutely nothing to do with camping, it does have everything to do with a journey—an unexpected detour might be more accurate.

I received a Facebook message, but not to my personal account. It was sent to my Honeysuckle Drive page. One of my followers was on her way to Canton, Georgia, and saw a cute little bakery and immediately thought of me. She thanked me for all my posts and bought me a coffee cup. This coffee cup! But, it would be about a week later before she would hand deliver it to me in my driveway.

During that encounter, we shared laughs and shed a few tears. She had recently lost her husband—her best friend, her rock. He had been in the hospital for a heart transplant. Everything was on the mend, and he was to be discharged the very next morning. She was finally bringing him home! But, God had a different plan. During his final night at the hospital, God called him home. Can you even imagine the shock? The disappointment? The heartache?

Yet, here she was in my driveway filling me with words of affirmation. Y'all, what a testimony! This woman, who has every right to be angry and bitter, chose kindness and joy. This woman, who has every right to be overly selfish, chose thoughtfulness. This woman, who has every right to never leave her bedroom, chose an abundant life. She is a fighter, and she makes broken look beautiful.

She shared with me how she had lived each day on autopilot, just kinda going through the motions. But, with the passing of her husband, she was forced into a different seat and with that different seat came a different view—a different vantage point. All these molehills that we turn into mountains are now ridiculously silly to her. Family, memories, time, purpose… that's what counts.

And, what was waiting for her in Canton? A cemetery. A visit with her husband. Y'all, I'll say it again. What a testimony! She is grieving a loss and giving to others at the same time. Her heartfelt story in my driveway changed me. Because of her, I'm on my phone less and in the moment more. Because of her, I'm chasing my purpose with a bit more passion. Because of her, I'm sipping my coffee this morning with a grateful heart.

It's not every day you witness someone use their pain for a greater purpose. It's not every day you witness someone turn their struggle into strength. We have no excuse. Life. Make it count—even when it hurts.

*　　*　　*

"He heals the brokenhearted and binds up their wounds." Psalm 147:3

*　　*　　*

We've all lost someone close to us. Who was your person?

_____

_____

_____

_____

_____

_____

_____

How do you honor his/her memory?

_____

_____

_____

_____

_____

_____

_____

How will you make today count?

_____

_____

_____

_____

_____

_____

_____

Day #5

Lemons

In classic Monday morning fashion, the "check-engine-soon" light started flashing across my dashboard, so my Ford truck is now in the shop. We all know what that means. All those rainy days that I've been saving for are about to get cashed in. While I was waiting for my ride, I decided to do a little window shopping. What could it hurt?!? Nothing but my pride! Holy Cow, trucks are expensive these days! They're about the equivalent of "my first home" in Carrollton, Georgia, circa 1994. But, I sure would look cute driving a jacked-up, white F-250.

I can just see me now. I'd have my windows down, country music blaring, cruising around Winder happy as a pig in mud until my daddy caught wind of what I did. I might be close to fifty, but he'd still cream my corn over such an extravagant purchase. I just don't get it. Doesn't the Bible state, "My Father wants me to have the desires of my heart?" Not my earthly father! I can tell you that right now. Ha.

But, guys, I do want a jacked-up truck… with tan leather seats, a sunroof, and WeatherTech floor mats. And, it's gotta be white, the kinda white they make you pay extra for. And, it's gotta be a Ford. I love me a Ford… unlike this little foreign rental I'm driving right now. When you're used to a truck, this rental feels like a go cart. I think I can… I think I can…

But, here's the take away today, folks:

Life happens and lemons are thrown our way—sometimes under-handed and sometimes in the form of a 90 mph fastball to the face. It's what we do with those lemons that shape us (and those around us). You can chunk them back at people. That might make you feel better. You can make lemonade. That's sweet. Or, you can put them in your bra and get a little extra attention. Whatever you choose, just remember: tomorrow is a new day! Thank you, Jesus!

* * *

"…Weeping may stay for the night, but joy
comes in the morning." Psalm 30:5

* * *

How do you handle life when it throws you lemons?

_____

_____

_____

_____

_____

_____

What does a "new day" mean to you?

_____

_____

_____

_____

_____

_____

Day #6

Ugly Words

My youngest son and I joined a mountain bike club that expects us to bike a total of 70 miles at designated state parks in Georgia.

Recently we bit off more than we could chew. I knew we were in trouble when the park ranger said, "Wow! No one's been on that trail since December." But we forged ahead anyway… eating spider webs and pushing our bikes more than we rode them. Fallen trees blocked a great deal of our path. It was scorching and the bugs were out. In fact, they were turning us into two-piece chicken dinners. I'm pretty sure one of my chigger bites has now turned into a flesh-eating virus.

The entire experience was awful. At our steepest climb my son said, "Mama, I'm about to say an ugly word." And, I could feel his pain. I was mighty disgruntled too. Our situation warranted an ugly word, probably several of them. He then asked me, "Well, can I say it?"

My bad attitude wanted him to shout it, but my heart knew better. I simply asked him, "Will saying an ugly word change our situation?" He quickly replied, "No," and continued humming while pushing his bike uphill.

When we made it to the top, there were no pretty views or cheers from the stands. It was just us—exhausted, discouraged, and covered in sweat. We then decided to say a simple prayer: Lord, may we return to our truck in record time. In Jesus' name, Amen.

And, here's where the trees parted revealing a paved path straight to the parking lot. Ha! Not really. We both proceeded to fall off our bikes once and a part of Bo's bike even fell off. We thought we would never make it out alive, but we did. When we finally reached our truck, there was much jubilation. We even celebrated with Dippin' Dots from the park office.

If we had known what was waiting for us on the other side of that bridge, we would have turned back without hesitation, but we would have also missed some valuable lessons.

1. Ugly words may be warranted, but they are not needed.
2. Prayer doesn't fix a situation, but it does make it bearable.
3. Gnats, mosquitos, and chiggers are from the devil.
4. There is great joy in overcoming obstacles.
5. Never let a stumble be the end of your journey.

* * *

"Those who control their tongue will have a long life; opening your mouth can ruin everything." Proverbs 13:3

* * *

Describe a time when you let your mouth get the best of you.

_____
_____
_____
_____
_____
_____
_____

What did you learn from that experience?

_____

_____

_____

_____

_____

_____

How do you apply that lesson when dealing with others?

_____

_____

_____

_____

_____

_____

Day #7

Call on Jesus

Have you ever hit a bump in the road that veered you off course? Sure. We all have. Has that bump ever landed you in a ditch? Possibly. Being in a ditch is much like being stuck in a rut. You're not getting out until you call for help. And when you're in over your head, there's only one person you can call: Jesus! He brings hope, and that's often all you need.

But, here's the deal, folks. I'm not getting outta that ditch without Him. That's why He's the easiest to cling to when I'm in over my head. He's the easiest to love when I need Him the most. Ain't that so selfish of me?

But, I fall short on my good days, too. On those days when I'm on time, traffic is smooth, and my workload is light. On those days when I'm eating healthy, the laundry is done, and my children aren't being difficult. On those days that are easy and routine. I don't need to praise Jesus now; I've got this on my own. Ain't that something else?

I'm pretty sure this makes me a fair-weather friend. I'm also pretty sure this qualifies me as a lukewarm candidate totally deserving of being spewed from His mouth. Fortunately, Jesus loves this hot mess! He knows how hard I'm trying to navigate life, so He shows me mercy and grace when I deserve it the least.

Rule #1 for Christians: When you know better, you do better! My love for Jesus should never be based on my need to be rescued. A friend loves at ALL times! And, what a friend we have in Jesus!

"Lord, help me to praise your name on both my good and bad days. Help me to seek you first in all that I do. Thank you for second chances at getting it right. In Jesus' name, Amen."

* * *

"I will praise you, Lord my God, with all my heart; I will glorify your name forever." Psalm 86:12

* * *

Describe a time when you've veered off course.

_____

_____

_____

_____

_____

_____

How did Jesus help get you back on track?

_____

_____

_____

_____

_____

_____

_____

Do you talk to Jesus more when your life is hard or when your life is good? Why is this?

_____

_____

_____

_____

_____

_____

_____

What can you learn from a detour?

_____

_____

_____

_____

_____

_____

_____

Week Six

Mustard Seeds

So, when was the last time you held a mustard seed in the palm of your hand? It's probably time for you to do this again. Why? Because that's all it takes, folks. Faith the size of a mustard seed. But, sometimes life can be mean and our faith takes a hit. That's when we must cling to God's promises the tightest.

> "Your faith is very important. I have done the math, and you are going to be dead a whole lot longer than you will be alive." Zig Ziglar.

Dear Lord, when doubt creeps in and fear trumps my faith, remind me of your promises. Your plans are far greater than mine. Help me to trust my situations when peace and understanding are not within my grasp. In Jesus's name, Amen.

PRAYER JOURNAL

Who will you pray for this week? What situations need God's guidance? Where does Jesus need to intervene? How can the Holy Spirit help? Date it and state it! Pray for these things each day this week. Update it as needed.

Day #1

Prepare Your Fields

Perhaps many of you have heard the parable preparing for rain. There were two farmers who desperately needed rain and BOTH of them prayed for it. But, only ONE of them went out and prepared his fields to receive it.

Which one do you believe truly trusted God to send the rain?

This story reminds us that FAITH is an action word.

In other words, trusting God doesn't mean I sit around and "wait" for something to happen. It means I get busy about the task at hand and prepare my field, whatever that may be, for God to deliver.

What "field" do you need to start preparing for a bountiful harvest?

Our prayers are powerful, but it is our FAITH that moves mountains!

*   *   *

"For we walk by FAITH—not by sight." 2 Corinthians 5:7

*   *   *

What are your biggest worries right now?

How could more faith make you worry less?

How can you grow your faith?

Why is it so important to be strong in faith?

_____

_____

_____

_____

_____

_____

_____

How can your faith help others?

_____

_____

_____

_____

_____

_____

What are the consequences of not having faith?

_____

_____

_____

_____

_____

_____

Day #2

Dangerous Distractions

So, I shared a post on my Facebook page that my sweet hubby saved my life this past weekend. I was on fire… sorta, just a little bit, and he put it out. Am I slightly exaggerating? Possibly. But, he saved me nonetheless.

It was nighttime. The game was on mute and my favorite song was playing. I was sitting by a campfire in the middle of nowhere—which means I was well below the gnat line in South Georgia (Montezuma to be exact). I may or may not have been sipping an adult beverage. But, everything about the moment was perfect. It had been a great day. The weather was wonderful, and the Dawgs had won big. So, I guess it's safe to say I was caught up in the moment.

That's when my husband comes barreling out of our camper practically charging at me. At that moment, I was on high alert and scared to turn around. I just knew a rabid coyote was gonna be behind me (When you're camping in the middle of nowhere, that's a high possibility, folks). And then he shouted, "You're on fire!"

"WHAT?!?!?!?!?!"

That's when he started swatting at all the sparks that had gathered on my right shoulder. Ouch! But, the crazy thing is, I didn't even know. I was so caught up in the moment that I had failed to notice I was in trouble.

I'm pretty sure the devil works just like that, folks. He distracts us with worldly things. It's when we're not paying attention that we become vulnerable. Let this post also be a reminder to get yourself some Godly friends—ones who have your back when you're not even looking. They'll end up saving your life.

But in this situation, my husband acted a lot like Jesus.

Jesus sees what we don't, folks.

He's always there: to answer prayers, to prevent danger, to discipline his followers, AND to keep us from burning... in hell.

The world gets so noisy it often drowns out Jesus's voice. He's there, folks. He's always there. Renew your mind and listen for Him.

*   *   *

"Instead, let the spirit renew your thoughts and attitudes.
Put on your new nature, Created to be like God—
truly righteous and holy." Ephesians 4:23-24

*   *   *

What things does the devil use to distract you?

_____

_____

_____

_____

_____

_____

_____

{Discernment: the ability to judge well} Why is discernment so important to your faith?

_____

_____

_____

_____

_____

_____

_____

How can you use your faith to tune out the world's noise?

_____

_____

_____

_____

_____

_____

Day #3

In the Valley

Y'all, this post ain't gonna mean a hill of beans to many of you. You're feelin' fine. But, to the person who needs to hear it, it's gonna be golden.

> It's okay to feel sad…
> and angry…
> and anxious…
> and afraid…
> and discouraged…
> and disappointed…
> and defeated.

The world makes us believe these are all terrible emotions and we are somehow "bad" if we feel this way.

Well, that's poppycock!

I hope you know that.

These feelings are a natural part of life… an ebb and flow of emotions. Highs and lows. Peaks and valleys. Sometimes we're the bug. Sometimes we're the windshield.

But, honestly, if it weren't for the valleys, some of us would never talk to Jesus. Think about that for a minute, folks.

Those valleys serve a mighty, mighty purpose. It's where we learn strength, determination, and perseverance. It's where we experience faith firsthand.

The Bible says a mustard seed of faith can move a mountain. But, the mountain doesn't need to move. We do!

God knew the valleys would come, but He never meant for us to sit and wallow there. He's beside us as we walk through the sadness, the anger, and the anxiety. He comforts us as we push through the discouragement, the disappointment, and the defeat.

There used to be a famous country song that said, "If you're going through hell, keep on going."

But, many people don't remember the most important next line, "Face that fire. Walk right through it."

We don't have to have it all figured out to move forward. Just take the next step. And another one. And another one. You can do this!

*   *   *

"Even when I WALK through the darkest valley, I will not be afraid, for you are close beside me. Your rod and your staff protect and comfort me." Psalm 23:4

*   *   *

Describe a time when you experienced a valley.

_____

_____

_____

_____

_____

_____

How did the experience draw you closer to God?

_____

_____

_____

_____

_____

_____

_____

Day #4

"In-Tents" Weather

I'm currently living in a tent. It's also a fairly new tent for me and my boy. And now that we've been on the road a while, we're kinda haphazardly setting it up. Maybe haphazardly is not the best word. It's just so second nature now that it requires zero thought.

So, needless to say, when a strong thunderstorm woke us up during the middle of the night, I had my doubts. Did I stake each pole? Did Bo hook the rain fly? Did I latch it around the poles? Is this tent even water resistant? All kinda doubt creeps in during a storm, folks. But, I failed to ask myself the one big question: Had I prayed for God's protection? The answer is YES!! We pray together each morning (and at night) for God's favor, protection, and traveling mercies. But, when I was caught up in the storm, I threw that out the window. I was trying to control the situation. Did I do everything right? Oh, ye of little faith! Fortunately, I serve an awesome God who loves me in spite of my doubts.

Y'all, that rain fly was like the armor of God. The wind blew. Our tent shook. The downpour sounded like a freaking hurricane. It was dark and frightening outside. But, not inside… that's where God kept us safe, and warm, and dry, and well-protected from the enemy.

So, here's your short and sweet: When you put on the full armor of God, you're telling the devil that he's gotta go through Jesus first to get to you… and we already know who wins that battle. Pray without ceasing, folks.

Amy Bowdoin

* * *

*"He alone is my rock and my salvation; He is my
fortress; I will not be shaken." Psalm 62:6*

* * *

Explain a time when you doubted God.

_____

_____

_____

_____

_____

_____

We all face storms. What's been your toughest battle?

_____

_____

_____

_____

_____

_____

Explain a time when you boldly wore the armor of God.

_____

_____

_____

_____

_____

_____

_____

Day #5

Aunt Evelyn

I know I've written a lot of stories about my grandmother. Well, she had an older sister. Her name was "Aunt Evelyn," and I sure did love her. When I think of her, sooooo many fond memories flood my mind.

She lived at One Bailey Drive, and she grew the most beautiful flowers. I especially admired her blue hydrangeas. They were so colorful and full of fluff. Her yard was also the first place I ever saw "Elephant Ears."

She was the first person to make me a fried bologna sandwich, and it tasted heavenly, folks. She was also the only person I have ever known to drink buttermilk. (And, yep. I still think that's pretty gross.) She introduced me to sponge baths and the comfort of falling asleep with a hot water bottle.

She knew baking soda could clean anything, and she was mighty resourceful. There was no need for fancy rain boots if you recycled your bread bags. She was a crossing guard for years, so dry shoes were kinda important. If your car was lacking heat or air conditioning, no problem! A thin piece of styrofoam across the ceiling would protect you from the outside temps. You wanna know what else would protect you? A paper grocery sack filled with empty aluminum cans. She placed it by her door at night as a homemade alarm system. If an intruder dared enter, he would spill the cans all over the floor and wake her. What she would do next, I have no clue. But, she wasn't worried because she was strong as an ox in her faith. However, she was no Motel 6. She was not about to leave any lights on—like ever. Or the TV, or the fan, or anything that didn't need to be on. She was not gonna waste anything, even power.

She believed in democracy or else she would not have volunteered to "work the polls" every single election. She could play the heck outta the piano, and she was always so darn calm and never in a hurry. She could make the 30 minute car ride from Carrollton to Newnan last a solid hour, and I'm not even kidding. It used to drive me nuts. Now that I'm older, I can appreciate the joy she found in not rushing to the next event. She truly savored the moment she was in, and that's something a lot of us have forgotten how to do. She made the most delicious tea cakes and pecan pies, and she always gave the most practical gifts.

One time she even hid all my daddy's underwear. True story! He was packing for a week long hunting trip to Colorado. She saw his stack of undies and simply put them away in his drawer. She thought she was helping with the laundry. He never checked his suitcase until it was too late. He swore my mama did it on purpose. Oh, we laughed and laughed. Guess what she gave him for his next birthday? Yep, she had a sense of humor, too.

She taught me that hot water and Dawn can get rid of ant mounds, walking outside was good for the soul, and to always save my egg shells. She would crush them up and keep them in her watering can. That had to have been her gardening secret. As she watered her flowers she would say, "Eggs shells are good for everything but walking on." I didn't get what she meant back then, but I sure do now.

My Aunt Evelyn has been on my mind all week. When I asked my mom how long she had been gone, she told me it will be 20 years next week. Ain't that crazy?!? It's been 20 YEARS and her memory is still golden to me. There will never be a statue, national holiday, monument, or scholarship named in her honor, but her legacy continues. How is that even possible?

It's because she took the time to plant seeds in a garden she'd never see. She wasn't rushing (life) along with an endless to-do list. She was savoring the moment she was in, and everyone knows… SAVORED MOMENTS NEVER FADE!

So, what's today's big take away?

SLOW DOWN!

Another hectic work week is coming for you, but it's giving you 10,080 minutes to use at your discretion. You can rush right through it OR you can plant some seeds. But, know this… You can't rush something you want to last forever.

*   *   *

"Be very careful how you live—not as unwise but as wise—making the most of your time, because the days are evil." Ephesians 5:15-16

*   *   *

Who in your family is your "Aunt Evelyn?"

_____

_____

_____

_____

_____

_____

_____

What seeds has this person planted in your life?

_____

_____

_____

_____

_____

_____

Life can get hectic. How do you savor the moments?

_____

_____

_____

_____

_____

_____

When was the last time you hit the pause button?

_____

_____

_____

_____

_____

PS: It's probably time to hit that button again.

Day #6

The Blue Door

Lemme tell you a quick story.

We spent our quarantine days remodeling our backyard. It was a labor of love that required countless hours and lots of blood, sweat, tears, a few ugly words, and some alcohol. The last thing we did was paint. My heart wanted a blue door, but my head was too scared to pull the trigger. What would people say? A white or black door would be a safe choice, but it just wasn't what I wanted.

So, I did what any girl would do. I asked my best friends and got the affirmation I needed. "Go with your heart. Don't ever look at that door with regrets." So, I painted it the most beautiful patriotic blue, and I've LOVED it! But then, my mom came for a visit and changed everything!

Oh, don't get me wrong! She loved the door, too. There's something mighty inviting about that blue door, but it was her comment that got me thinking. We're sitting there, slowly rocking, when she says, "That door brings you such joy. It's a shame you can't see it every day. You've gotta wait until you're sitting in your backyard." Well, guys, that was all it took. The seed was planted, and I fertilized it daily by constantly thinking about it. It took me all of one week, and the deed was done. My pantry door now mimics my back door. But, I love it! And now it brings me joy all day long. It's only a little paint. No harm. No foul. I could have it back white by tomorrow night.

Well, that's it. That's my quick story. Did you see what just happened? Like me, you probably didn't notice it either. I better explain…

Please, please, please continue to put on the full armor of God and guard your heart! Just like that, my mama planted a seed and walked away. I did the rest myself. I cultivated it, and I fertilized it until I was ready to act. BUT, what if that seed hadn't been a harmless paint color? What if that seed had been negative opinions about our beautiful country, our strong police force, our brave military, our need for justice, or vaccine mandates? We are bombarded with "seeds" non-stop via social media, the news, and our neighbors. Without the full armor of God, how can we truly discern fact from fiction or truth from fake news? We can't, and that's what gets us into trouble. Now more than ever guard your heart and dig your heels deep, so that you can stand firmly on the promises of God. If we reap what we sow, we better be strategic in what gets planted.

*   *   *

"Above all else, guard your heart, for EVERYTHING you do flows from it." Proverbs 4:23

*   *   *

How do you prevent the wrong seeds from being planted?

_____

_____

_____

_____

_____

_____

Why is this so important?

_____

_____

_____

_____

_____

_____

_____

What are the consequences of NOT guarding your heart?

_____

_____

_____

_____

_____

_____

_____

Day #7

Miss Faith

I was born and raised in Carrollton, Georgia. I lived there for 34 years. I graduated from college there. I birthed two unbelievably awesome children there. I even taught school at the same school I attended as a 7th and 8th grader. The chances of me ever escaping were looking very slim. Heck, I had never even driven past Arbor Place Mall by myself, and that's a straight shot down I-20. To say my life experiences outside of Carrollton were minimal would be an understatement. Then one thing lead to another, blah blah blah, and I found myself remarried and moving to Athens, Georgia. (I'll save all those details for another story. Just know that life happens.)

It is now the summer of 2009. As a teacher, it's the most wonderful time of the year. As a newlywed, it's a pretty magical time, too. However, I was lonely, terribly lonely. (Please note: I was madly in love with my husband. This had nothing to do with him. This was about me.) I had left behind all I had ever known… two unbelievably awesome children who didn't want to move, a job of 13 years that I had loved, a comfy house, fantastic friends, a supportive family, my church, my favorite stores, and my sense of direction. I was now stuck sitting all alone inside a former bachelor pad from sunup to sundown. (Remember: It's summer and Bill was an extremely busy landscaper.) I could not even find the grocery store or Walmart. I was always getting lost and calling either Bill or his sister to guide me home. I was also terrified to start my new job. Teachers can be mean, and I didn't know who to trust or who would be able to put up with me, so I stayed to myself. I was puzzled. How could I be so blissfully happy with my husband yet feel so lonely at the same time? I now had two choices: I could continue to wallow in loneliness, or I could do something about it. I opted for choice #2 but primarily because the word wallow makes me think of pigs, and I did not want to be referred to as a porker.

My first bright idea was to join some sort of junior women's league. That would force me to socialize and gain new friends. I contacted my local women's league and prepared to wait. Little did I know, there is protocol that must be followed; one cannot simply just join and start contributing. I had to reside in Athens for one year, be invited to join by a current member, and prove myself worthy. Say what?!? I may be a bit country, but I'm not crazy. I quickly realized this would NEVER be the group for me. Exclusive has never been a characteristic high on my list. So, I decided they were the ones not worthy of me, my creativity, or my compassion. And, I continued to sit… again… all alone. And, that's when it hit me: a thought from my youth days at church. I would "adopt" a grandmother.

I started researching local nursing homes and made my choice. I selected the nursing home with the worst reviews and the most write-ups. I figured they were the one that needed me the most. I would call and ask to volunteer. It was located right down the road. I wouldn't get myself lost trying to get there. Ha. The whole process was relatively easy. The office staff paired me with a lady whose son had abused her and left her lying in a bed, in her own feces, while he cashed all her social security checks. The son, her only family member, was in jail and she was a ward of the state. Therefore, absolutely no one ever came to visit or check on her. Her name was Faith, also known as "Miss Faith", and I was about to be her best friend. I visited her twice a week for about an hour. This lasted for a good year, and our meetings were always the same.

> "Hi, Miss Faith, do you remember me? No.
> Well, I'm Amy and I'm here to read you a book."
> "Hi, Miss Faith, do you remember me? No.
> Well, I'm Amy and I'm here to paint your fingernails."
> "Hi, Miss Faith, do you remember me? No.

Well, I'm Amy and I brought you chocolate."
"Hi, Miss Faith, do you remember me? No.
Well, I'm Amy and I'm here to sneak you outside."

I think you get the idea. Our greetings were the same, but by the end of the hour, I couldn't keep her quiet. She would fondly tell stories of her childhood growing up in Arkansas. Her parents owned a store near the railroad, and her father would leave shoes (for needy children) on the doorsteps of their houses during the night. It was always meant to be a surprise gift, but he was a dead giveaway because he owned the local store. He would always deny it and refuse to ever let the parents pay him back… unless the mother could bake a good pie. We need more people like Miss Faith's father… people who spread kindness and charity without ever seeking credit for it. Miss Faith couldn't have children of her own, so she adopted her only son. And, despite his cruelty, she continued to speak so highly of him. A mama's love knows no bounds. Then one day she started talking about her brother. He had been a missionary in Kenya his entire adult life until he retired. He was married with two daughters… and his two daughters happen to be quite famous. (I bet you didn't see that one coming.)

If you are a close friend of mine, you know how I like to play detective and boy, did I have my chance. I started researching, calling, emailing, etc… to get in touch with these two daughters. I shared my great discovery with the nursing home manager and got the shock of my life. I was told that I could not let her family know her whereabouts. It was nursing home policy. You have got to be kidding me?!? She needs her family. She wants her family, and I have to just sit here and say nothing. Ha! I think not. And, here's where those who really know me, know my panties were all knotted up. I was ticked! I have never handled "no" too well. I launched my own campaign to reunite Miss Faith with her family. I contacted, via email and letters, every local official, state official, news organization, and basically anyone with a title that might help me. While I did receive a bunch of lip service, I also received a phone call from then Governor Sonny

Perdue's secretary (and within 24 hours of submitting my email to him). The Governor was so moved by my email that #1. He gave me permission to contact her family and #2. He appointed me to his staff. LOL! Well, he had me report to my local Ombudsman Services Department. I underwent an interview, completed a background check, and was given my official name badge and clipboard. I now had "the power". My badge and clipboard gave me permission to walk into any nursing home in the state of Georgia and fight crime… to fight injustices done to one of our most precious resources: the elderly.

Everyone had been experiencing budget cuts and setbacks. The Ombudsman Services Department was not immune. At the time, there were hundreds of nursing homes in my region and only a few people to inspect them. My assignment was totally voluntary, but I did have to document all my hours and report in each week with my discoveries… an elderly man with the same soiled shirt on three days in a row, an emergency call button that had fallen to the floor out of reach from the elderly woman stuck in her bed, a dry water cup with no straw that had sat on a nightstand all week, etc… I was an advocate for the elderly, and I LOVED it! I was no longer lonely. I had a greater purpose.

Finally, I was able to reach the famous author by email and she forwarded all my information to her father, who was Miss Faith's only brother. He called me that night and I was able to reconnect him with his sister. It appears Miss Faith's son would not let them talk to each other on the phone, so he had no idea what had happened to her. He could not believe she was a ward of the state. Within a week, he and his wife flew here from Missouri to reunite with Miss Faith. It was fantastic. They could not afford to relocate her to Missouri (Plus, there was a lot of red tape with her being a ward of the state), but she now had a family that called her once a week and sent her a monthly allowance for snacks. They also flew back to visit her about every 6 weeks. Mission accomplished.

It's at this point in my story that I become a bit selfish. I was loving my job at my new school and that kept me busy. Bo was now crawling all over the place, and I felt guilty leaving him at daycare all day and again in the evenings so that I could visit with Miss Faith. I also got scared that I was going to make Bo sick. There were several times when the entire nursing home was quarantined due to flu and everyone was always just so sickly. So, with a saddened heart I had to resign from my governor appointed duty. (Governor appointed – Ha! It makes me sound special.) I could no longer devote the time it so desperately needed from me. My visits with Miss Faith slowly dwindled from twice a week, to once a week, to once a month, to maybe once a quarter, and eventually I stopped going all together. I'll never forget my last visit with her. It went something like this…

"Hi, Miss Faith, do you remember me? No.

Well, I'm Amy and I'm here to sing you some songs.

A nurse who was helping Miss Faith's roommate spoke up and said, "Oh, you're Amy. I'm glad I can finally meet you. Do you see that baby doll on Miss Faith's bed? A local church gave it to her for Christmas. She talks to it all the time. She named it Amy."

And, that's when I knew that life is not coincidental or accidental. It is well planned and crafted.

You see, I serve a God who knew Miss Faith needed someone to help her reunite with her family.

I serve a God who did not abandon me during my time of sadness and loneliness, for He knew—all I needed was "Faith".

Amy Bowdoin

*   *   *

"Faith can move mountains." Matthew 17:20

*   *   *

How has your faith saved you from wallowing?

_____

_____

_____

_____

_____

_____

_____

What does it mean to have faith that God has a purpose for you

_____

_____

_____

_____

_____

_____

_____

What are some ways God could use you to accomplish good/ do his work?

_____

_____

_____

_____

_____

_____

_____

Week Seven

On Hold

I've had to wait 45 minutes at a restaurant just to get a table for dinner. I've been placed on hold even longer than that with customer service. Waiting is the worst. But, it's especially excruciating when we don't know when the waiting will end. Patience is hard for me. And, sometimes, trusting God's plan is even harder. Fortunately, God will never forget us or forsake us. We are in good hands... even when his answer is wait.

> *Dear Lord, help me to accept my wait time. Fill me with patience and positivity. Make my heart content with not knowing and not being in control. Give me the ability to wait without worry because your plans are better than my own. In Jesus's name, Amen.*

PRAYER JOURNAL

Who will you pray for this week? What situations need God's guidance? Where does Jesus need to intervene? How can the Holy Spirit help? Date it and state it! Pray for these things each day this week. Update it as needed.

_____

_____

_____

_____

_____

_____

_____

_____

_____

_____

_____

_____

_____

_____

_____

_____

_____

_____

_____

_____

_____

Day #1

First Buck

This is NOT what I had planned to write about today, but here we are… venturing off course just to prove a point.

I recently shared how we skipped school to go hunting, and it proved to be quite a productive and memorable weekend. One for the record books for sure… Bo's 1st buck!

Oh, their celebratory pic could have made the cover of any outdoor magazine. A proud father and son. A moment one of them had dreamed of for over twenty years—a son following in his dad's footsteps, loving the great outdoors and the thrill of the hunt. But, please don't think they got here overnight, folks. Seeds were planted many YEARS ago!

That 10 year old deer-slayer was once a 2 year old little boy. He wore camo, carried a toy gun, and made as much noise as possible in the stand. But, his daddy waited patiently, carefully pointing things out… like proper gun safety, the direction of the wind, scent control, body language, knowing your target, the importance of letting one mature… all of it. The next year it was more of the same. Year after year and nothing. But, that daddy was patient. Most hunters are. He kept coaching, encouraging, and planting seeds.

They played target games in the backyard. They watched hunting shows on TV. They studied the anatomy of a deer and how to score the rack. And then one day, out of the blue, that daddy's faithfulness was rewarded. That little boy, who had previously had the attention span of a squirrel, had grown into a young man who loved the great outdoors and the thrill of the hunt. Mission accomplished!

But, guys, the day you plant the seed is NOT the day you eat the fruit!

My husband waited for this moment (and patiently prayed, hoped, dreamed, and poured himself into this moment) for 8 YEARS! But, my hubby is not alone. Abraham waited. Sarah waited. Moses waited. Joseph waited. Jesus waited.

We must trust God even when His answer is "wait." And, if I've learned anything, it's this: NEVER underestimate what God is doing in your season of waiting.

Today's lesson: You take care of the sowing;
God will take care of the growing.

*   *   *

"Wait patiently for the Lord. Be brave and courageous. Yes, wait patiently for the Lord." Psalm 27:14

*   *   *

Waiting is so hard. What are you tired of waiting for?

_____

_____

_____

_____

_____

_____

_____

What seeds are you planting in others?

_____

_____

_____

_____

_____

_____

_____

What seeds are you planting in yourself?

_____

_____

_____

_____

_____

_____

_____

Day #2

Longing for More

So, here's the deal.

Once upon a time, I thought I was dying. With one bad test result, I learned how fragile life can be. But, that moment was a much needed shock to my system.

It made me very intentional with my time, my words, and my energy. It also ignited a fire in my heart. My need for adventure was through the roof and kayaking Lake McDonald at Glacier National Park was #1 on my bucket list. And, marking that off my list quickly became my mission.

I saved money. I stockpiled goods. I planned. I mapped. I Googled. I practiced. I did "all the things" to make it a reality. And, it only took me 6300 miles and 33 days in a tent (with my baby boy) to make it happen. Talk about a trip of a lifetime!?! That was it.

BUT… that was this past summer, folks, and now I'm in a pickle. My heart is restless, and my daily routine only makes it worse. Compared to my summer, everything I do seems so stagnant.

So, I find myself just going through the motions. Where's the passion in that?

There is none.

So, what's a girl to do?

My mom believes my desire for a more gypsy lifestyle is quite juvenile and maybe she's right—she usually is. So, I pray, and I specifically pray for discernment. How else does one distinguish between a selfish want and a genuine longing for more?

As I searched for answers last night, I stumbled upon this quote from Jennie Allen. "There is one answer to your soul's deepest thirst: Jesus."

I know I was created for more, but I'll never get there without Him. He is the way, the truth, and the life.

*   *   *

"Come to me, all who are weary and burdened,
and I will give you rest." Matthew 11:28

*   *   *

What's on your bucket list?

_____

_____

_____

_____

_____

_____

What consumes your thoughts while you wait for it to happen?

_____

_____

_____

_____

_____

Explain how you plan to turn your bucket list into a reality.

_____

_____

_____

_____

_____

_____

_____

What's Jesus's role in that plan?

_____

_____

_____

_____

_____

_____

_____

Day #3

Sweet Surrender

"Are you there, God? It's me."

I know it's been a minute.

I've been tired—just so tired.

Tired of wanting.

Tired of wondering.

Tired of worrying.

Tired of wishing.

Tired of waiting.

I didn't wanna think... or do laundry... or cook dinner... or buy groceries... or workout... or help with homework... or drive a kid to practice... or go to work... or deal with people... or watch the news... or attend that event... or be thoughtful or nice.

None of that.

I just wanted to sit on the couch.

That's it.

I wanted to sit there and inhale the moment while exhaling my problems.

I know what you're thinking.

It does sound kinda selfish and lazy, but it's soooooo much more than that. I promise.

While I was sitting there, I learned something. I learned there's a mighty big difference between surrendering and giving up.

Giving up means you're done. Game over!

Surrendering means you're letting go… so God can work.

** Strength does not come from always winning. **

Trust God's timing and God's plan. He knows how your story ends.

Today's lesson: Sometimes it's not the times you fight—but the times you surrender—that make all the difference.

*   *   *

*"Be still before the Lord and wait patiently
for Him to act." Psalm 37:7a*

*   *   *

Explain a time when you needed a break—a timeout.

_____

_____

_____

_____

_____

_____

If you could surrender two things, what would they be?

_____
_____
_____
_____
_____
_____
_____

Where do you feel like giving up?

_____
_____
_____
_____
_____
_____

What would it look like to surrender instead?

_____
_____
_____
_____
_____
_____

Day #4

The Reluctant Reader

Y'all, hell might be freezing over.

I can't even believe this mess myself. But, last summer I watched a series on Netflix called Sweet Magnolias. It's a total chick flick that takes places just outside of Charleston, South Carolina. My favorite part is the fierce friendship between the women on the show.

Well, imagine my surprise when one of my BFFs told me it was originally a book, AND she had it in her possession. Say what? This is the same book I posted about during spring break. It took me almost a year to finally pick it up to read it. Why? Well, I hate to read. I really do, so I tried to avoid it. But, it kinda seems like the thing to do when you're basking in the sun.

So, I dove into book #1 and absolutely loved it. I'm fairly certain it was because I had watched the show first. The characters were so real in my mind. When I got to the end, I discovered another shocker. It is a series that contains twelve books.

So, I went straight to Amazon and filled up my cart. I was the proud owner of books #2 through #4. And, like a good teacher, I had book #4 with me during state testing. I'd make a few laps around the classroom and then read a few pages of my book. Anything to pass the painfully slow time. Well, I eventually got to a part in the book I wasn't prepared for. I'm pretty sure it would have made the author of *50 Shades of Grey* blush. What in the world?!? I could not believe I was reading this in the middle of state testing, but it did cause me to pick up my pace as I canvassed the room. I'm also pretty sure I power-walked all of section 2 with a smile. All I know is, when testing was over and I had access to a computer, I immediately ordered books #5, #6, and #7. Bwaaa Haa Haa!

But, I write all this for one reason. I'm 46 years old, and I have hated reading for 46 years. But, look at me now, folks! I am newly converted, and all it took was some sultry words printed on a page.

But, seriously, you've been praying for somebody for a long time. That somebody might even be you. And, you're getting tired. Tired of waiting. Tired of hoping. Tired of praying. Tired of nothing happening. Don't stop believing in the desires of your heart. Don't stop believing in change or in a miracle.

Joseph waited 13 years.

Abraham waited 25 years.

Moses waited 40 years.

And, my mama waited 46 years… for me to enjoy reading.

If God is making you wait, you're in good company. Time changes everything, folks!

Keep the faith.

*   *   *

"And let us not grow weary of doing good, for in due season, we will reap, if we do not give up." Galatians 6:9

*   *   *

Who are you steadfastly praying for?

_____

_____

_____

_____

_____

_____

What's the best way to pass the time while we wait?

_____

_____

_____

_____

_____

How can waiting grow your faith?

_____

_____

_____

_____

_____

Day #5

He's Waiting on You

Hello. My name is Amy, and I might have an online shopping problem. And, I'm totally blaming it on the pandemic. Why not? We're blaming everything else on it, right?

But, I think Amazon is ah-mazing! One click. That's it. And that mess is already on its way. But, what really gets me going is when it states, "Order within the next 2 hours to get it tomorrow." Tomorrow? Say what?!? How do they do that, folks? I'm pretty sure it's some sorta voodoo or black magic, but they've totally ruined me. I have lost my ability to wait, and in 2020, that's like the most important life skill to have.

Waiting on dinner	Waiting on an email	Waiting in traffic
Waiting on quitin' time	Waiting for a vacation	Waiting for the weekend

Waiting for the next season of *Sweet Magnolias*—Ha!

But, then it gets harder.

Waiting on test results	Waiting for an apology	Waiting on Mr. Right
Waiting for normal to return	Waiting on a cure	Waiting for a baby

But, here's something I've learned in my short forty-six + years: Waiting is never a waste of time! Why? Because HE'S in the waiting!

He's waiting on you…

>   to lean
>   to trust
>   to pray
>   to hope
>   to dream
>   to believe

"Just because God isn't talking to you about the problem doesn't mean He isn't working on the answer." Instead of getting flustered or frustrated, increase your faith!

It only takes a mustard seed to move a mountain. Just imagine what you could do with a peanut. You could change the world!

*   *   *

> *"You, too, must be patient. Take courage, for the coming of the Lord is near." James 5:8*

*   *   *

What is God waiting on you to do?

_____

_____

_____

_____

_____

_____

How can you increase your faith?

_____

_____

_____

_____

_____

_____

_____

Day #6

Looking for Butterflies

You're not gonna believe this!

I spent the majority of my summer break living in fear. It wasn't until I totally surrendered my heart (while having three biopsies) that I received my blessed assurance—total peace with whatever the outcome may be.

The waiting game was the worst part of the entire process. My mind likes to race when I'm waiting, and it really likes turning minor molehills into insurmountable mountains. I doubted myself and God's ability to take care of me. I allowed fear to trump my faith. But, God brought me to this mountain—not to upset my life—but to remind me how to climb. And, He answered my prayer with cancer free results the day before I was to climb a real mountain with my husband for our anniversary. That's more than a coincidence, folks. That's God.

Our hike to the top of Mount Mitchell was one for the record books. It was breathtakingly beautiful and incredibly challenging. Once we reached the summit, we were filled with emotion. We will never take our health or each other for granted again. Naturally, we wanted to capture this moment, so we asked a stranger to take our picture. When she returned our camera she asked, "Want me to take another one? I think a bug was in it." I glanced at it and told her it was just fine how it was. In fact, it was more than fine. It was perfect—a kinda perfect that could only be orchestrated by God himself.

Now I must rewind time just a bit. In 2006, my wonderful mother-in-law lost her battle with cancer. When our youngest son was born, in 2010, my husband and I made a promise that Bo would know his

"YaYa." One day, when he was two years old, we were walking outside and saw the prettiest butterfly. Bo told us it was YaYa, and that's just sorta stuck with our family. Every time we see a butterfly, one of us says, "Hi, YaYa." Or, "Look! There's YaYa." Or, "YaYa is checking up on us again." Or, my favorite is when Bo comes home from school and says, "I saw YaYa today on the playground." Butterflies symbolize grace, joy, goodness, and promise (to us). But, we never expected to see one at an elevation of 6500 feet. And, what are the odds it would resemble the tiny butterfly I had tattooed on my right shoulder blade almost 15 years ago? Folks, God has planned every detail of our life. Don't miss His fingerprints on the pages of your days.

The butterfly is proof that you can go through a great deal of darkness and still be beautiful. Don't quit before the miracle happens! In a world that gets crazy complicated at times, never stop looking for butterflies.

*   *   *

"Open my eyes so that I will observe amazing things from your instruction." Psalm 119:18

*   *   *

Explain a time when you allowed fear to trump your faith?

_____

_____

_____

_____

_____

_____

What mountain has God asked you to climb?

_____

_____

_____

_____

_____

_____

Describe a time when God gave you a "God-Wink."

_____

_____

_____

_____

_____

_____

_____

Day #7

The Right Door

I teach at a middle school five minutes from my house. When I get there, I prefer to park in one of the end spots. Why? I'm lazy and I don't want to walk far to the door. Ha.

There's a certain door that grants us entry with our keycard, so naturally that's the end spot I'm going for. But, recently I noticed the door at the end of that same hallway is always open. Like every time, folks. Hmmm… I think I'll start parking on that end. It's less congested. So, that's exactly what I did on Tuesday morning.

But, when I got to the door, it was closed and locked. "Are you kidding me?" That sucker had been open for two weeks. Fortunately, someone was standing nearby that could let me in. When I explained what I was trying to do, she confirmed my thoughts. That door IS always open. However, the next morning, I didn't want to risk it. I went back to the old door on Wednesday, and what do you know? When I looked down the hallway, that other door was wide open. Geez!

So, on Thursday, I thought I would try it again. I even watched another teacher walk around the corner. Great! It's open. But, as I approached the door, the door was locked and that teacher was huddled in the corner attempting to seek shelter from the rain. And, it gets worse. No one was nearby to let us in. OMG! Why?!?!

So, on Friday, I wasn't doing that again. I entered through the original door, looked down the hallway, and yep! That crazy door was wide open. Can you believe that mess?

Clearly that's not my door, folks. And, I've wasted a lot of valuable time trying to enter it. We won't even discuss all my frustrations. I've been so super-focused on that one door, that I failed to notice all the other opened ones. But, there's a great lesson here.

If God shuts a door, stop banging on it! We pray for Him to direct our path and then get frustrated when we're inconvenienced. A closed door is a huge blessing—especially when danger lurks outside. Trust God's plan! The right door will open soon, and then everything will make perfect sense. It's all part of God's perfect plan for your life.

*   *   *

*"I have placed before you an open door that
no one can shut." Revelation 3:8*

*   *   *

What doors have God closed in your life?

_____

_____

_____

_____

_____

_____

Which door did you keep banging on before you got the message?

_____

_____

_____

_____

_____

_____

Which door could not have been opened without God's help?

_____

_____

_____

_____

_____

Closed doors remind me of unanswered prayers. Do you ever thank God for unanswered prayers?

_____

_____

_____

_____

_____

_____

Which unanswered prayer are you most thankful for?

_____

_____

_____

_____

_____

_____

_____

Sticks and Stones

"… but words will never hurt me." What a big fat lie that was! Our words are mighty powerful weapons. And, while we do have the ability to forget the words, we don't have the ability to forget how they made us feel. And, once our feelings get involved, life gets pretty complicated.

> *Dear Lord, please help me to be mindful with my tongue. Let me pour out life-giving words onto my family and friends. Put your hand over my mouth when I start to spew venom and negativity. Also, strengthen my backbone when others share their words with me. Give me the wisdom to know what's true vs. what's coming from negative emotions. We all say bad things when we're hurting. Help me to love them through it. In Jesus's name, Amen!*

Week Eight

PRAYER JOURNAL

*Who will you pray for this week? What situations need
God's guidance? Where does Jesus need to intervene? How
can the Holy Spirit help? Date it and state it! Pray for
these things each day this week. Update it as needed.*

Day #1

Don't Believe Everything

So, I stumbled upon a quote on a friend's Facebook page the other day, and it really resonated with me.

"Be careful what you hear about someone; you might be hearing it from the problem."

Folks, that's a mouthful right there.

If my daddy or my brother said it to me once, they said it a thousand times. "Don't tell me that." And, they'd both be shakin' their head in disbelief. I'd merely be sharing something I had heard from a "friend" and they'd both be astounded that I even believed it. So, what they were really saying to me was, "Don't tell me (you fell for) that?" [Insert blank stare here because I DID!] And, the conversation would always end with, "You're too naive." But, they were right.

Not one time did I ever check my friend's sources. Not one time did I ask for a 2nd opinion.

Not one time did I question the motive. Not one time did I compare track records.

Not one time did I ask to hear the other side of the story.

So, was I naive? Probably. And dumb, and gullible, and way too trusting. Not one time did I ever doubt what I had heard. I just accepted what was said at face value and used that exaggerated information to form a very tainted opinion of my own.

But, I was wrong, folks. Dead wrong. This only became more obvious once I became the topic of the conversation vs. an innocent bystander/listener.

It was about this time (middle school to be exact) that my mama gave me some tips for surviving life. She knew I would be eaten alive if she didn't intervene. These tips even saved my sinking ship a time or two in high school. It's not top secret information. But, here's the crazy part. They apply whether you're a scrawny twelve-year-old girl or a slightly overweight forty-seven year old woman.

1. Those who gossip to you will soon gossip about you. Tread lightly around those people.
2. No matter how carefully you choose your words, they'll always get twisted by somebody. Share your truth regardless.
3. People are quick to believe the bad things they hear about good people. Do good anyway.
4. Live in such a way, that if someone spoke badly of you, NO ONE would believe it.

That #4 is the ultimate mic drop. If you are truly living according to God's will, then you have nothing to fear and nothing to explain (or justify). Let your character and what you stand for speak for itself. Your friends already know the truth, and as a follower of Christ, you know the truth, too.

*   *   *

"Gossip is spread by wicked people; they stir up trouble and break up friendships." Proverbs 16:28

*   *   *

Think of a time when you have jumped the gun and believed the gossip before hearing both sides. What steps can you take to not stir the pot?

_____

_____

_____

_____

_____

_____

_____

How would Jesus handle gossip?

_____

_____

_____

_____

_____

_____

_____

Day #2

Your Yuck is My Yum

I'm not gonna lie. When it comes to my baby boy, I'm pretty biased. I think he's an awesome human. Well, I used to think that before Halloween made him greedy.

That little joker went trick-or-treating with friends and racked up on the candy. He came home and immediately started spreading it out on the kitchen counter. I assumed he was gonna give me the pick of the litter. Nope. He started forming two distinct piles. When he was done, he said, "You can have everything in this pile."

"Awe. That's so sweet."

(AND, here's where he ruined it, folks.)

"Yeah, that's all the candy that I don't like."

Where's the love in that? Where's the personal sacrifice for my happiness?

All I could say was, "Wow. And to think, you used to be my favorite child."

And, here's where I got schooled by a 6th grader.

"Do you like peanut butter cups?" Yes!

"Do you like Almond Joys?" Yes!

"Do you like plain M&Ms?" Yes!

"Well, that's what's in your pile."

"Do you like Tootsie Rolls?" No!

"Do you like Laffy Taffy or Gobstoppers?" Not even a little bit.

"What about Milk-duds?" Absolutely not!

"Well, that's what's in my pile. Don't you get it, mom?"

And, here was the best line of the day…

"Your yuck is my yum, and that's okay."

Let that line sink in a minute, folks.

Your yuck is my yum, and my yum is your yuck… and THAT'S OKAY!

Lord, have mercy! How many times have I faked liking something to fit in with the crowd?!? Too many!

I don't like Chick-Fil-A like most people. I'd much rather have Bojangles. That's blasphemy, right?!? I can't go around hatin' on the Lord's chicken. But, it's the truth. And, while I'm only mentioning chicken to keep the mood light, we do this same sorta thing with politics, sports, which church we attend, which schools our children attend, the tennis shoes we wear, the neighborhood we live in, our thoughts on vaccine mandates, abortions, etc…

So, here's today's lesson: Don't allow society to turn you into a person you're not. What makes you different is what makes you beautiful. Being real is the greatest filter you could ever use. Trust me!

Today's goal: It's not about being all the same. It's about respecting someone's yuck when it's not your yum.

*　　*　　*

"Don't copy the behavior and customs of this world, but let God transform you into a new person by changing the way you think. Then you will learn to know God's will for you, which is good and pleasing and perfect." Romans 12:2

*　　*　　*

Explain a time when you faked something to fit in with the crowd.

_____

_____

_____

_____

_____

_____

_____

Explain a time you followed the crowd and regretted it.

_____

_____

_____

_____

_____

_____

_____

What is something you really enjoy that others don't?

_____

_____

_____

_____

_____

_____

What makes you different?

_____

_____

_____

_____

_____

_____

Day #3

Failure is Never Final

So, I had "the talk" with my boy this weekend, and if you're thinking birds and bees, that was a few summers ago. And, that conversation was easy.

This conversation was about all my "failures"—hot messes that I found myself in while growing up. Some were all my fault and others were just bad timing.

We discussed all the late night sneaking out just to meet up with his daddy—and we only got caught once, folks. I'm pretty proud of that.

We also discussed:

> Beer drinking and wine coolers
> Cigarettes in my nightstand drawer
> Late night, unsupervised parties
> Failing math with a 56
> Not making the team
> Multiple spring breaks in PCB
> Getting excluded by "friends"
> So much gossip
> So much pressure
> So many bad decisions
> Getting pregnant in high school
> My depression and needing help
> A failed first marriage

We even discussed one party (in college) where this guy started doing lines of white powder on the coffee table and you wonder how you landed in that moment. AND, you specifically wonder how you're gonna get yourself out… which was the entire purpose of this conversation. Everyone needs a lifeline—especially our children.

It was important—to me—for Bo to know I've been there. I have failed. I have made some serious mistakes. I have hit rock bottom more than I care to admit, but you get up, you dust yourself off, and you keep pushing forward. There's no other option.

> No mistake is too big.
> No situation is too messy.
> Failure is never final.
> Disappointment is never permanent.

He can always, ALWAYS, count on his mama… no judgements and no questions until the morning (He embraces my nosiness, folks).

We also discussed his fears, his dreams, college and even marriage and kids. This weekend was rich in conversation and most definitely needed. Middle school and high school are boogers to navigate—especially these days.

And, no, I'm not trying to be his friend. I'm his parent—an honest one. He knows my expectations. I expect his best—his personal best. But, at the end of the day, I'd much rather him be real than fake perfection. That mess is exhausting.

Mental battles are fought at all ages and for a variety of reasons. Be present. Be easily accessible. And, be ready to listen. Growing up is tough.

[Note: It blows my mind when parents pretend to be perfect. I believe it's the biggest disservice one can do. And now I'm slowly stepping off my soap box.]

*   *   *

"CONFESS your sins to each other and pray for each other so that you may be healed..." James 5:16

*   *   *

What are some things you'd like to confess?

_____

_____

_____

_____

_____

_____

_____

Describe a time when you hit (or were close to) rock bottom?

_____

_____

_____

_____

_____

_____

_____

Would you rather people be messy or perfect? Why?

_____

_____

_____

_____

_____

_____

_____

How does sharing our failures bring us closer together?

_____

_____

_____

_____

_____

_____

_____

Day #4

Progress, Not Perfection

So, I lost a follower yesterday.

She was highly offended by a post. She was appalled that I would reference *Fifty Shades of Grey* and scripture in the same post. She was even more appalled when I told her I've been known to cuss a little and overindulge in Fireball Whiskey. <clutches pearls>

I suppose she'd rather me pretend to be someone I'm not. But, I've played that role before, and it's exhausting. It's also what gives Christians a bad name.

Hypocrite: 1: a person who puts on a false appearance of virtue or religion. 2: a person who acts in contradiction to his or her stated beliefs or feelings.

I've confessed from day #1 that I'm the least qualified to share scripture. And, after all this time, I still don't know all the books of the Bible. I'm no saint—far from it, folks. But, I love the Lord with all my heart, and I AM willing… to be transparent, to share my struggles, and to seek God in all I do. I also believe God loves broken people. Scratch that. I kinda think He prefers them.

But, she's proof that we are not gonna be everyone's cup of tea, and that's okay. But, if you think about it, do we really wanna be for everyone? No. I've made that mistake before, too. It's not good to morph into whoever you're around. Before long, you forget who God has called YOU to be.

And, yes, I can handle constructive criticism. Have you ever met my mama? I was raised on it, folks. But, what I do have a hard time handling is someone who has lost her ability to take a joke. Life is too short to skimp on the laughter.

I am not as good as I wanna be, but thanks to God, I'm sooo much better than I used to be. Strive for progress—not perfection, friends. "Be who God created you to be, and you will set the world on fire."

*   *   *

"For I know the plans I have for you," says the Lord.
"They are plans for good and not for disaster, to give
you hope and a future." Jeremiah 29:11

*   *   *

Describe a time you offended someone with your words.

_____

_____

_____

_____

_____

_____

Have you ever pretended to be someone you're not?

_____

_____

_____

_____

_____

_____

How did that work out for you?

_____

_____

_____

_____

_____

_____

_____

Who has God called you to be?

_____

_____

_____

_____

_____

_____

_____

Day #5

Whatever!

I've taught middle school for 25 years. I've been a mother for 28, and I've been a daughter for almost 47. Trust me. I've said my fair share of eye-rolling "whatevers," and I've received my fair share, too.

Back in the day, "whatever" was the last word, and I usually mumbled it under my breath as I walked away. My mama thought it was quite disrespectful, and my butt sat home several weekends because of it. It wasn't until I got older (and wiser) and much stronger in my faith that I realized "whatever" was a God-given lifeline.

My hubby would be the first to admit I'm sassy and a bit salty. My mouth has gotten me in more trouble than I can count on both hands. It's taken me a LONG time to learn that some battles aren't mine to fight; they're the Lord's. And, it's taken me even longer to learn that not everything requires my opinion. Silence can be more powerful than proving a point. But, the struggle is real! When you're a natural born talker, it's mighty hard not to shout from the rooftops.

So, I do what I've always done since turning 13 years old. I roll my eyes and mumble, "Whatever!" But, like I said before, what was disrespectful earlier in my life has now become my saving grace.

"WHATEVER!" It's my reminder to stay true, noble, and right.

"WHATEVER!" It's my reminder to stay pure, lovely, and admirable.

"WHATEVER!" It's my reminder, that when things head south, I don't have to pack a bag and go there with them.

"WHATEVER!" has become one of my favorite Bible verses of all time. (Yep, of all time!) I even had it printed on cups as a giant reminder to keep my cool when life gets chaotic.

Negative experiences (and people) are unavoidable. "Whatever!" keeps me from having to wash my mouth out with soap. It's also way more acceptable than saluting folks with my middle finger. For some reason, that mess is frowned upon. (But, the struggle is real these days, guys.)

"Whatever" is good for your soul... do that.

*   *   *

"Finally, brothers and sisters, whatever is true, whatever is noble, whatever is right, whatever is pure, whatever is lovely, whatever is admirable– if anything is excellent or praiseworthy—think about such things." Philippians 4:8

*   *   *

How do you handle negative experiences?

_____

_____

_____

_____

_____

_____

_____

What is good for your soul right now?

_____

_____

_____

_____

_____

_____

Day #6

You're Enough

When I look into a mirror, I can see all my imperfections and short-comings. I bet you do this, too. Why? Why are we so hard on ourselves? Our bodies hear everything our minds are saying, and that's a heavy burden to carry. Stop trying to fix yourself; you're not broken. You're fearfully and wonderfully imperfect.

You will never inspire people by being perfect. You inspire others by how you deal with your imperfections. It's time to lighten the load! You owe yourself the love you so freely give to other people. Imagine if we obsessed about the things we loved about ourselves. Talk about a mind shift!

So, if you're searching for that one person who can change your life, look in the mirror. Know who you are and know that you're enough! You're the child of the one true king.

*   *   *

The Lord said to Israel: "I have loved you, my people,
with an everlasting love. With unfailing love, I
have drawn you to myself." Jeremiah 31:3

*   *   *

What is one of your many strengths?

What is one of your best features?

What is something you are proud of? Why?

What makes you feel accomplished?

_____

_____

_____

_____

_____

_____

_____

How can you use these attributes to strengthen a friend's faith?

_____

_____

_____

_____

_____

_____

_____

What do you hope people remember about you?

_____

_____

_____

_____

_____

_____

_____

Day #7

Is it Me?

I've written lots of posts about my baby boy. He's twelve years old and brings me great joy. But, he's also all boy—an active, smelly boy.

It doesn't matter if we're sitting at the dinner table, driving in the car, or if I'm trying to relax in a hot bath.

"Mama, smell this." always finds me.

It could be stinky socks, shoes, armpits, or the aftermath of noises that came from his backside. But, like a good mom who's lost her mind, I always play along and smell it.

Yes, he wears deodorant.

Yes, he showers daily.

Yes, he brushes his teeth.

Yes, he even uses mouthwash.

Yes, he has tons of socks.

Yes, he has good shoes.

All the things are in place, so he's not the smelly kid. But, it happens.

Yesterday we were waiting at a traffic light, and Bo got a whiff of something foul. He was like a bloodhound trying to sniff out the source. Finally, in desperation, he asked, "Is it me?"

Folks, he was genuine and super serious, but the way he said it made me laugh out loud. He couldn't fathom the possibility that the foul odor might just be coming from him. But, that scenario got me thinking.

How many times have you found yourself in the middle of something unpleasant? Lots, right? How many times have you asked yourself if you are the problem? Not near enough!

It's hard to accept our part of a yucky situation. I'd much rather stick my head in the sand than have to deal with confrontation or my part in a mess. But, here's a little thing about denial. Denying the truth doesn't change the facts. Sometimes, even when it's not our fault, it's still our problem. That stinks, right?

People will go to great lengths to avoid what's real and painful inside them.

Let's not be those people.

*   *   *

"The end of a matter is better than its beginning, and patience is better than pride." Ecclesiastes 7:8

*   *   *

Be honest. What are you currently avoiding?

_____

_____

_____

_____

_____

_____

If you never address it, how will it ever get better?

_____

_____

_____

_____

_____

_____

Think about this question: Is it me?

_____

_____

_____

_____

_____

_____

That Girl

I have this vision in my head of who I really want to be. Sometimes I nail it. Sometimes I miss the mark. And, other times, I compare it to others and fall short…every single time. It's so hard to be who God has called me to be when the world is steadily demanding I be something else. Or, maybe just maybe, I don't trust God's plan for my life as much as I say I do. Please tell me I'm not alone.

> *Dear Lord, please help me to be that girl—the one who looks in the mirror and likes who she sees. The one who looks in the mirror and knows her worth without needing the world's validation. Give me ears that hear the truth and a mind that can easily tell fact from fiction. You set me apart for a reason. Don't let me give-in. In Jesus's name, Amen.*

PRAYER JOURNAL

Who will you pray for this week? What situations need God's guidance? Where does Jesus need to intervene? How can the Holy Spirit help? Date it and state it! Pray for these things each day this week. Update it as needed.

_____

_____

_____

_____

_____

_____

_____

_____

_____

_____

_____

_____

_____

_____

_____

_____

_____

_____

_____

_____

_____

_____

_____

Day #1

Wake with Purpose

Be the girl who wakes with purpose, walks with intent, and stands for truth.

Be the girl who smiles first, who speaks first, and who ALWAYS makes room for others.

Be the girl who shows up... with the Margaritas and chocolate when a friend is in need.

Be the girl who fights for injustice and who never cowers in the face of adversity.

Be the girl who is strong enough to forgive yet smart enough to remember.

Be the girl who keeps secrets and who never stirs the pot.

Be the girl who knows her light doesn't dim when she compliments others.

Be the girl who says the positive things when others are complaining.

Be the girl who believes anything is possible and who never stops dancing.

Be the girl who notices a need and who jumps into action without hesitation.

Be the girl who doesn't surrender to laundry, a hectic work week, or mindless gossip.

Be the girl who makes broken look beautiful and who shares her scars to help others find hope.

Be the girl who doesn't quit and who dusts herself off time and time again until she's proud.

Be the girl who raises other women up and never tears them down.

Be the girl who lets the petty stuff go and who walks away with pride.

Be the girl who goes for it, even when she's scared.

Be the girl who is filled with gratitude and lets the world know it.

Be the girl who gives—her time, her money, her energy, her smile, her hope—to help others.

Be the girl who is fearless in the pursuit of what sets her soul on fire.

Be the girl who balances life by making time for Jesus.

Be the girl who is a mighty prayer warrior for her family and friends.

Be the girl who is not afraid to stand alone.

We live in a fast-paced, CRAZY world where you can be anything you want. **BE THAT GIRL!**

*   *   *

"… She is more precious than rubies." Proverbs 31:10

*   *   *

Read that list again. Put an * by the ones that need improvement.

How are you gonna make that happen?

_____

_____

_____

_____

_____

_____

_____

Read that list again. Highlight or circle the ones you have mastered.

How can you use those strengths to glorify God?

_____

_____

_____

_____

_____

_____

_____

Day #2

If Only...

We all have that one thing.

If only…

If only…

If only my hair were longer, darker, straighter, thicker.

If only I were taller, stronger, or much thinner.

If only I had a nice car or a cute little house with the picket fence.

If only I got the promotion, offer, bonus, or raise.

If only my spouse would do that or Mr. Right would finally arrive.

If only I had something to look forward to or could take a vacation.

If only I had friends who blah, blah, blah.

Y'all, this list could go on, and on, and on, and on. There's ALWAYS that one thing that we think we're missing or needing. If we only had that one thing, our life would be perfect. And so, without it, we're just not as good enough or as worthy enough as others.

And, that way of thinking is absolute POPPYCOCK!!

I personally know a guy who believed you were to die for. I even know another who sacrificed his only son. Let those last two sentences really sink in, folks. Sometimes we forget we're royalty—a child of the one true king! We need to sashay into our day like a boss.

You are enough. You've always been enough.

Keep your head up! Otherwise, your crown might fall.

"In a society that profits from your self doubt, liking yourself is a rebellious act."

*　　*　　*

"I am fearfully and wonderfully made; your works are wonderful, I know that full well."
Psalm 139:14

*　　*　　*

What is your best quality?

_____

_____

_____

_____

_____

_____

How would your best friend describe you?

_____

_____

_____

_____

_____

_____

How would God describe you?

_____

_____

_____

_____

_____

Why is it so hard to believe these positive things?

_____

_____

_____

_____

_____

_____

Day #3

Son of a Biscuit!

Disclaimer: This is not a funny post. This is a momma-messed-up post. But, it happens, folks. Grace upon grace.

If you've been following me for a while, then you already know I went on a BIG trip last summer. You also know I ordered a new tent just for this trip. We needed a bigger one for when my husband joined us on our journey. Naturally we gave it a test run. I had to know I could assemble it myself—with some minor assistance from a ten year old boy.

We did all the things, folks. We counted the pieces. We laid them all out. We followed the directions… well, sorta. At this point in my journey, I'm a trained camping professional. The directions were meant for newbies, right? They're more like guidelines anyway. Nope. Nope. And nope. Thinking I was too cool, too smart, and too experienced was my first mistake.

For the life of me, I could not get the final pin through the last tent pole. I was mad as a hornet, and before I knew what happened, I shouted, "Son of a biscuit." But, I didn't say biscuit, folks. And, my child was standing right there in shock—absolute shock. I don't say ugly words in front of him, and if you'd have asked him BEFORE my tent fiasco, he would have told you I've maybe said ten ugly words my whole life. At 46 years old, that's about 2 ugly words a decade. Not too shabby! But now, AFTER my tent meltdown, he's bumped my count up to twenty-five.

"Son of a biscuit" is not even my ugly word of choice. I typically prefer a word that rhymes with spit. So, at this particular moment, I'm kinda in shock myself. Where did that even come from? But, I started wrestling that pole like it was a dadgum grizzly bear. And, also at this same moment, Bo's shock turns to belly laughs. Well, you know good and well that only makes me more mad. So, I said S.O.B. one more time just to up his count.

Eventually Bo questioned, "How long is Dad with us on this trip? Are you sure he's worth all this?" That's when I realized I was in over my head, folks. I told Bo, "Go get your Daddy before Jesus kicks me right outta heaven."

And, wouldn't you know it, my hubby snapped that pin to that pole like it was nothing. He also showed me a much better (and faster and easier and safer) way to do it. He even showed me in the directions where I had messed up. Skipping one minor step almost cost me my religion, folks.

Once I cooled down and my blood pressure returned to normal, I did have a chat with my baby boy.

"Did me saying those ugly words help my situation at all?"

"No ma'am."

"So, when I was in over my head, what saved me?"

"Asking for help."

"And, I'm gonna need you to remember THAT the rest of your life."

So, today's lesson is a simple one: Sometimes asking for help is the bravest move you can make.

Today's goal is much harder: Be strong enough to stand alone, smart enough to know when you need help, and brave enough to ask for it.

*   *   *

** For I am the Lord your God who takes hold of your right hand and says to you, "Do not fear; I will help you." Isaiah 41:13 **

*   *   *

Describe a time when you really should have asked for help—but you didn't.

_____

_____

_____

_____

_____

_____

_____

What made asking for help so difficult?

_____

_____

_____

_____

_____

_____

_____

Even good girls mess up. Describe a time when you wished you could have taken back your words—but it was too late.

_____

_____

_____

_____

_____

_____

God also promises to help us. What do you need His help with now?

_____

_____

_____

_____

_____

_____

Day #4

Big Booty Britches

So, I've been working out lately. And, by lately, I mean diehard, every day, for several weeks. After throwing away my scale, I feel fantastic. Actually, I feel better than fantastic. I feel like a million bucks. So, what did I do? I stepped up my game.

I got me a fake hair piece, a fresh coat of eyebrows, and lash extensions. (I mean… go big or go home, right?) And, I'm not gonna lie. Now I'm feeling like a million bucks AND feeling a heckuva lot younger, too. So, I can't stop now. Right? Right!

So, I ordered me a pair of those booty-lifting TikTok leggings. And, if you don't know what I'm talking about, a quick Google search will fill you in. I had almost given up hope they were even gonna arrive. It's been a few weeks since I'd ordered them. But, I got them in the mail yesterday… just in time to "lift" my spirits on a rainy afternoon.

Y'all, I was so hopeful. I was gonna be the cutest Kim Kardashian wannabe this side of the Mississippi. But, what a big disappointment! Those leggings don't lift squat. In fact, it's the opposite. My backside resembles a flat pancake with hail damage. How do I know? I made my 5th grader take a picture of it. Oh, no, no, no! This will never do.

It was about that time, I heard my hubby pull into the driveway. Thankfully, I HAVE been working out, so I was able to leap over the bed, rip off those britches, and hide all evidence that I had temporarily lost my mind before he walked in the door. Whew! Humiliation averted.

Now one might think today's post is about vanity, but it's not. There's nothing wrong with doing things that make you look and feel better about yourself. This post is about laziness. I wanted those leggings to instantly make me look like a rockstar without putting in the blood, sweat, and tears to earn it. Achieving one's fitness goals doesn't work that way. Life doesn't work that way. Relationships don't work that way. Wanna know what else doesn't work that way? Everlasting life.

I can go to Heaven without lash extensions or crazy leggings. I can even go to Heaven without reaching my goal weight. But, I can't go to Heaven without Jesus.

Today's Goal: There's a reason there's a highway to hell but only a stairway to Heaven. Exercise your faith by walking with Jesus—Every. Single. Day.

*   *   *

"... What does Christ require of you? To act justly and to love mercy and to walk humbly with your God." Micah 6:8

*   *   *

When was the last time you did something nice for yourself? What was it?

_____

_____

_____

_____

_____

_____

How did it make you feel?

_____

_____

_____

_____

_____

_____

Describe a time you followed a crazy fashion trend. Why did you?

_____

_____

_____

_____

_____

How do you exercise your faith?

_____

_____

_____

_____

_____

Day #5

Forecast: Answered Prayers

We made plans last week to visit Lake Russell on Sunday. With all the recent rains, I longed to be on the water and under the sun. The weather forecast did not look promising with a 60% chance of rain. Yuck! I joked with Bill that our attitude about the forecast would determine if we were a pessimist or an optimist. We both wanted to be the optimist, so we decided to focus on the 40% chance that we might just have a beautiful day.

8 AM arrived quickly and drearily. "It's all good. Let's go." And, just like that we were on our way to the lake. It was not long before it started misting, sprinkling, and outright raining on our car. "It's all good. We're going to a lake. We're supposed to get wet. Keep going!" We even had to make a special stop at Bojangles just to wait out the worst of the storm. It was while we were waiting that I asked Bo to pray for blue skies and warm sunshine. He enthusiastically did.

By 9:30 AM we were finally cruising the open water, and it was gorgeous... for about 15 minutes. "Hurry! Top up or top down? Where's my hat? Let's hide under a towel. Who's idea was this? Geez, Louise." It was then that Bo and I said another prayer. "Dear God, we need some blue skies." I'm pretty positive we said it a good 5 times. I was almost ready to throw in the towel when Bill spotted some blue skies. No one else could see them at all, but Bill promised us they were coming. And, he was right.

The remainder of our day was perfect! We had beautiful, blue skies, warm sunshine, calm waters, and great friends to enjoy it with. We stayed until everyone was sunburned (after 6 PM). That's a long day on the water, especially with a toddler. It wasn't until we were exiting the boat that Bo said, "Look at all that blue sky. God answered my prayer". He was so excited that he shouted the good news to his father. I pointed out to Bo that we are always very quick to ask God for favors. We need to be even quicker to thank him. He then shouted up at the sky, "Thank you, God and Jesus, for listening to me." My heart smiled.

It was while we were driving home that Bill and I discussed the awesomeness of our day. God listened to Bo, and Bo knew it!! "God answered my prayer." We are trying to instill in Bo that God is always there for him to talk to. We could not have planned a better example for him to witness. As I rode in awe of our tiny miracle, I allowed doubt to creep in. "Was it really God? What are the odds? I'm no meteorologist, but it could have been wind currents and good luck." It was at that very moment that I spotted Taco Bell. (My family will testify. It has always been my favorite place to eat.) I glanced at their sign, and my jaw dropped. I should have stopped and taken a picture. It did not advertise the latest burrito special. It simply read, "God is able." On a Taco Bell sign? You better believe it!

So, you see… the day's lesson was not intended for Bo but for me.

God works in mysterious ways. He knows Bill and I are competitive. He knew if we challenged each other to be optimistic about the weather that we would drive to the lake in a hail storm. God knew we had been diligently practicing prayers with Bo. He knew praying for blue skies would be obvious and a simple prayer to answer. God also knew that I would allow doubt to taint our miracle, and he squashed that doubt with a quickness. I can now thank Taco Bell for reminding me that God listens to me, too. He doesn't just listen to cute little boys with blue eyes. He listens to me… someone often confused, slightly broken, a little selfish, full of mistakes, but filled with potential and a desire to know Him. Great is thy Faithfulness!!

Honeysuckle Drive

*   *   *

*** *"If you believe, you will receive whatever you ask for in prayer." Matthew 21:22* ***

*   *   *

Describe a time when you know God answered your prayers.

_____

_____

_____

_____

_____

_____

How did this make you feel?

_____

_____

_____

_____

_____

_____

What about when God's answer is no? How does that make you feel?

_____

_____

_____

_____

_____

_____

_____

Day #6

Happy Lights

I'm an (early) morning person. I love being the only one awake while the rest of the house is sleeping. There's something sacred in the stillness. It's when I do the majority of my thinking, praying, writing, and talking to God.

Here lately my mornings have been missing some magic. What is so different? And then, it hit me. My Christmas lights are gone! Being the good daughter that I am, I had all of my Christmas decorations properly put away by January 1st. No bad luck here! But, those twinkling lights made me happy. Why would anyone box-up and store away their happiness until next year?

So, at 6 AM on Sunday morning, I tiptoed to the basement in my nightgown and located our garland and two strands of lights. I had everything in position and was sipping coffee on the couch by 6:20 AM. It was heavenly! But, at 7:15, here came my hubby.

I fully prepared myself for a "What in the world, Amy?" But, instead I got a "That's cool!" And, at 8:30 AM, my baby boy finally woke up. His response, "Yes! I've missed those lights." Ain't that how it usually goes? I was dreading their reaction—because the world thinks those lights belong in a box until next Christmas—but, they are my people! They love the magic of those lights as much as I do.

We've been in the dark and missing out all because why? Because the world says Christmas is over. Well, poppycock! Even when Christmas is over, the Light of the World is still here! Our lights are back on, people. Mama is feeling rebellious. But, I'm also feeling all warm and fuzzy as I sip my coffee this morning. Hallmark would be proud.

How long will they be up? Who knows? It could be forever, or they could come down as early as next week. Who am I kidding? Those jokers are on display through my birthday. Ha! They're called "happy lights" now and happiness isn't seasonal.

You deserve to be happy. You deserve to live a life you're excited about. Don't let the world make you forget that!

*   *   *

"No one lights a lamp and then puts it under a basket. Instead, a lamp is placed on a stand, where it gives light to everyone in the house. In the same way, let your good deeds shine out for all to see, so that everyone will praise your heavenly Father." Matthew 5:15-16

*   *   *

Whose voice do you listen to most: yours or the world's? Why?

_____

_____

_____

_____

_____

_____

_____

Describe a time you dimmed your light because it was too bright for others?

_____

_____

_____

_____

_____

_____

_____

Why is it so difficult to be fearlessly authentic?

_____

_____

_____

_____

_____

_____

How do you tune out all the noise?

_____

_____

_____

_____

_____

_____

Day #7

Putting in the Work

People post a lot of crap on Facebook. When this happens, I usually think, "Oh, bless their heart!" And, I just keep scrolling and minding my own business. There's no way I'm jumping in that political arena or Super Bowl circus.

But, sometimes you come across something so profound, so convicting, that you screenshot it and store it in the vault. That happened to me recently.

How many times have I prayed for something? A LOT, right? How many times have I assumed God said no, or was absent, or wasn't listening? Several!

But, what if God wasn't avoiding my request? What if He was equipping me with everything I needed? Hmmm…

"People pray for cake… Then God gives them the batter, the oil, a pan, an oven, and the icing, They get frustrated waiting for cake to magically appear, so they leave the kitchen in search of something else."

Oh, ye of little faith!

Nothing in life is free! Noah didn't wake up and find a boat sitting in his front yard. That joker worked hard to make it happen and did everything God asked him to do. If God is working on my behalf, I've gotta be willing to work with Him.

If I pray for God to move a mountain, I better be prepared to wake up next to a shovel. And, you better be prepared, too! Be the girl willing to work for it!

Amy Bowdoin

* * *

"Work willingly at whatever you do, as though you were working for the Lord rather than for people." Colossians 3:23

* * *

What are you currently praying for?

_____
_____
_____
_____
_____
_____
_____

How are you helping God make this happen for you?

_____
_____
_____
_____
_____
_____
_____

Where are you putting in the work?

_____

_____

_____

_____

_____

_____

How long are you willing to work for what you want?

_____

_____

_____

_____

_____

_____

PS: Don't stop until you're proud.

Week Ten

Cattywampus

Every now and then when I'm at the gym, my coach has us do this exercise. She wants us to stand on one leg while doing bicep curls. It seems simple enough until we start. The tiniest of things will cause us to lose our balance: a fly, a piece of hair flapping in our face, sweat, you name it. In order not to fall, we have to put down our other leg for support. Once we regain our balance, we start again. Life kinda works this same way. The tiniest of things will cause us to lose our balance. To keep from falling, we lean on our friends, family, and faith for support. Once we regain our balance, we start again. But, here's what my coach taught me. If you want a strong sense of balance, you need a strong core. In life, our core is a heart for Jesus.

> *Dear Lord, when my life gets out of control, help me to stay calm and anchored in your word. Give me the confidence to hit the pause button, so I can reset my attitude. Please help me keep my priorities in order and my ducks in a row. In Jesus's name, Amen.*

PRAYER JOURNAL

Who will you pray for this week? What situations need God's guidance? Where does Jesus need to intervene? How can the Holy Spirit help? Date it and state it! Pray for these things each day this week. Update it as needed.

Day #1

Nothing Blooms All Year

Life Tip: ALWAYS find time for the things that make you happy to be alive!

I know what the Bible verse states: I can do all things. But, it doesn't state: I can do ALL things ALL the time. And, there's a big difference there.

We live in a society that glorifies being busy. We run here, there, and everywhere with an endless to-do list of expectations and obligations. No wonder we feel like we're drowning! But, nothing blooms all year, and that includes you. So, quit foolin' yourself! You don't always need to be getting stuff done. You've gotta fight for the balance, and that balance includes time for yourself!

When you take time to replenish your soul, it allows you to SERVE OTHERS from the overflow. (Remember: We are here to serve—not to be served.)

So, here's the deal: It's okay to be busy like Martha as long as you stop to rest (at His feet) like Mary!

So, invest in rest... or hikes, or chocolate, or fishing, or shopping. Whatever floats your boat keeps you from drowning, and you kinda need more of that. Make time for the moments you can't put into words, folks. That time will change your life!

*   *   *

"But Martha was distracted by the big dinner she was preparing. She came to Jesus and said, "Lord, doesn't it seem unfair to you that my sister just sits here while I do all the work? Tell her to come and help me." But the Lord said to her, "My dear Martha, you are worried and upset over all these details, but there is only one thing worth being concerned about. Mary has discovered it, and it will not be taken away from her." Luke 10:40-42

*   *   *

What brings you joy?

_____

_____

_____

_____

_____

_____

How do you create a healthy balance?

_____

_____

_____

_____

_____

_____

What needs to change for you to invest more time in yourself?

_____

_____

_____

_____

_____

_____

_____

How are you gonna make this change a priority?

_____

_____

_____

_____

_____

_____

_____

Day #2

Living with Intention

I was a much nicer person in my late 20s and early 30s. I went out of my way to do for anyone and everyone—sometimes at the expense of my own family.

I never missed a gathering, a birthday, a sporting event, or a chance to be needed. I had this unfounded idea that more was better: more friends, more obligations, and more demands. I spent every moment giving more and more of myself away. I was busy doing a whole lotta nothing, folks—absolute nothing. And that kinda nothing feels more like drowning than success.

But, I blinked and everything changed.

I woke up in my mid-40s only to realize that time was fleeting. Overnight "more" became a four-letter word. I didn't want more of anything. Less was best! Less friends, fewer obligations, fewer demands—and less drama! My circle of friends may have drastically dwindled, but its worth grew exponentially. I no longer needed a legit reason to decline a social obligation. The fact that I didn't want to go was reason enough. I wasn't being rude; I was being intentional.

"Living with intention means saying no to the things that aren't important to us so that we can say yes to what matters most."

It's hard to do things that set your soul on fire if you're stuck at Karen's 3rd baby shower. Honestly, I can't believe it took me over 40 years to figure this out.

Making my needs a priority is not selfish. Caring for myself is not self-indulgence. It is self-preservation. And, guess what? It makes me fierce!

When you've spent your whole life listening to others, it takes courage to pay attention to the sound of your own voice.

You had a purpose before anyone had an opinion. And, you'll never fulfill that purpose if you're always busy with trivial things. You can be a good person with a kind heart and still say no.

As kids, we were taught to say no to drugs. As adults, it's imperative that we say no to the unnecessary.

Be intentional, folks. Time is not refundable.

*　　*　　*

"Teach us to number our days, that we may
gain a heart of wisdom." Psalm 90:12

*　　*　　*

What is consuming the bulk of your time?

_____

_____

_____

_____

_____

_____

_____

How can you rearrange your schedule to allow more time for things that bring you joy?

_____

_____

_____

_____

_____

_____

_____

How do you make time for Jesus?

_____

_____

_____

_____

_____

_____

What sets your soul on fire?

_____

_____

_____

_____

_____

_____

Day #3

You, Me, Us

You can tell by my face this activity was not my choice at all. I made the mistake of committing to the ride before I had tested the waters. And, you know how it goes with kids.

"Again! Again! Again!"

It was right up there with getting a root canal, folks. The slide was fine. It was the crash landing into a pool of 40 degree water that I couldn't take. I wasn't a big fan of climbing stairs to the top in a bathing suit either. But, we were just outside Custer State Park in South Dakota. The mountain views were incredible and a sight to behold for this Georgia peach. As we waited in line for our turn, I told Bo, "At least the wait is beautiful." And, do you know what that little joker said?

"It sure is… just like you, mom." (Insert sigh here.)

Had it been anyone else, I'd have called him a schmoozer, a real Casanova. But, as I turned to look at him, he was as genuine and as sincere as he could be. And, there's only one person he gets that from, folks—his daddy! So, I proceeded to go down that frigid slide and risk hyperthermia a hundred more times. Wouldn't you?

But, since we've been on our road trip, we've developed a pretty strict rule: you, me, us. It's that simple. We do one thing he likes—even though we both know I'm gonna hate it (like an ice cold water slide). We then do something I'm gonna love—like hiking to the top of a mountain on a hot day. But then, we pick an activity we both wanna do—like riding a horse and ending the evening with ice cream. There's only so many monuments and trees a 10 year old can enjoy.

I want this to be a great memory for the both of us. So... it's you, me, us. That's what us old folks call a win-win. It's also what I call a beautiful compromise.

If you're not willing to bend, sooner or later you're gonna break... and it's the breaking that hurts. Life is a journey. It's okay to share the driver's seat.

*   *   *

"Do not forget to do good and to share with others, for with such sacrifices God is pleased." Hebrews 13:16

*   *   *

What areas of your life need a compromise?

_____

_____

_____

_____

_____

_____

We all have that one non-negotiable. What's yours? Why?

_____

_____

_____

_____

_____

_____

How do you share the driver's seat with others?

_____

_____

_____

_____

_____

_____

_____

Day #4

Icy-Hot

So, I've officially hit middle age, and I kinda feel like I'm falling apart. I often joke with my hubby that about this time is when most men would trade me in for a newer model. I'm very fortunate he's not like "most men."

But, when I get out of bed, my bones creak much like opening an old car door. I don't have any rust peeking through my paint job, but I do have grey in my hair. My headlights no longer point straight ahead; those high beams now point at my feet. At this point, I'm what you'd call "Old Reliable." She doesn't quite run like she used to, but you can't part with her just yet.

But, I'm working on it, folks. I'm at the gym each morning at 5 AM trying to keep the wheels from falling off. Sometimes that causes me to lift a bit heavier than I should. And, when this happens, "Old Reliable" depends on "Old Faithful." He'll bring me the Ibuprofen, massage my back, and place my Icy-Hot patch in just the right spot. I'm not real sure what's in those things, but, man, they feel good. I should know. I wore one all weekend.

And, that got my brain to thinking. Is it cold or is it hot? It's soooo hard to decipher what I'm feeling, but I've experienced this before.

I once had a friend. We were pretty close, but something just wasn't right. I could sense it. Sometimes she'd be great, and friendly, and super supportive. Yet other times I had to watch my back. She'd be the first one to push me in front of a moving bus. When it was good, it was really good. But, when it was bad, it was bad, folks. She was just like that Icy-Hot patch. I never really knew if she liked me or hated me. My heart wanted her to be my friend, but my head knew better. So, I eventually found the courage to cut the cord, and my life has been better for it.

This same thing happened to me with my faith. One minute I was on fire. I would read my Bible each day, I never missed church, and I was always doing for others. And then, I fell off the wagon. I traded reading my Bible for scrolling through Facebook. I started sleeping-in instead of getting my butt to church. This nonchalant attitude affected all areas of my walk with Jesus. I had become that lukewarm Christian He detests so much. I had to break some serious chains (and bad habits) to get my life back on track, but I sure am glad I did. I'd hate to "almost" be a Christian and "almost" get into heaven.

And, all these memories were brought to you courtesy of one Icy-Hot patch. But, my "friend" taught me a valuable lesson. Just because it feels good, doesn't mean it's good for me. And, just because it's good for the moment, doesn't mean it's good for eternity. You can't be a part-time Christian and demand a full-time God. It just doesn't work that way, folks.

*   *   *

"Because you are lukewarm, neither hot nor
cold, I will spit you out of my mouth!"
Revelation 3:16

*   *   *

Are you hot, cold, or lukewarm for Jesus? How do you know?

_____

_____

_____

_____

_____

Which area of your life needs a bit more heat? Why?

_____

_____

_____

_____

_____

_____

_____

A healthy balance is so important. Where are you falling short?

_____

_____

_____

_____

_____

_____

_____

Day #5

Shaking Things Up

I am so embarrassed to admit this, but that's never stopped me before.

Once upon a time, I used to be the queen of clean. Now I've really settled down. Who am I kidding? I hit my forties and quit caring. Cleanliness is just not high on my list of priorities anymore, but I do work at it from time to time. So, on Saturday, I started wiping counters. No biggie! But then I made my way to my kitchen table. What in the world?!? Guys, I love my crazy-busy Walmart placemats, but these jokers have been holding crumbs hostage for days. I had just eaten breakfast at this very table. There was no need to be alarmed. I noticed nothing! But, the moment I shook one… watch out!

I took a pic of the moment for documentation because I knew this realization would be too hard to believe. I looked perfectly normal (and healthy and cute) on the outside, but on the inside, I was a mess, folks… and I didn't even know it. But, Lord, after I shook things up I noticed. That entire pile of crap had been camouflaged within my placemats. It was weighing me down, and I didn't even know it. I took care of it and now my table is sparkling like never before. It's a much happier and healthier table now.

Here's the wild part. God does this to us all the time. We think we're fine. We think we've got everything under control, and then BAM!! He shakes up our life. Many times we think we're being punished, but that could not be further from the truth. God is shaking things up because He can see what we can't. He knows what's weighing us down and keeping us from our purpose, so He helps us get rid of it. He wants us happier and healthier, but sometimes it takes surviving an earthquake to get us there. Be willing to shake things up to make things right!

*   *   *

*"Consider it pure joy, my brothers and sisters, whenever you
face trials of many kinds, because you know that the testing
of your faith produces perseverance." James 1:2-3*

*   *   *

When was the last time you experienced a trial of Godly proportion?
What was it?

_____

_____

_____

_____

_____

_____

_____

What did that experience teach you?

_____

_____

_____

_____

_____

_____

_____

Day #6

Switching Gears

So, yesterday I did a thing. I dusted off my Trek mountain bike and went for a trail ride at a phenomenal state park just 5 minutes from my house.

At this point in my biking career (I sound so official), I've biked over 200 miles. This was not my first rodeo by any means, but it had been a couple months. I can blame it on the weather, my son's new scooter interest (Yep, I have a scooter, too), or the fact that I'm a mom. We get busy and life gets in the way. Regardless, yesterday's ride was long overdue.

My hubby gave me the greatest gift. He stayed home with our son who is still recovering from the flu, so I could ride solo... just me and my bike. The weather was darn near perfect and, oddly enough, no one else was on this part of the trail. It was just me, the woods, a beautiful lake, a slight chill in the air, and some heavy panting. This heifer is outta shape. But, God was there, too.

As I was biking, I was asking Him how I could use this experience on my blog. I REALLY thought this was going to be a post about not delaying our happiness, making it a priority. I absolutely LOVE riding my bike. I've missed it. I feel so alive when I'm riding, but then...

I hit some quicksand. With all this rain, there are some super soggy patches on the trails. It slowed me down to molasses. No biggie! But, right ahead of me was a steep incline. I'd never make it up the hill without some mojo. So, I started pedaling as fast as I could, but it wasn't enough. As I hit the hill, I had a middle-age brain fart. For the life of me, I could not remember which way switched my gears from high to low. Mama here hit the wrong one. I might as well hit the brakes. I had to jump off my bike and walk to the top. Such defeat!

But, I kid you not, the moment I reached the top God said, "There it is. There's your topic."

Y'all, I'm an experienced mountain biker—over 200 miles of experience. I have a fantastic bike and the best gear. I had everything I needed to be successful, but when I was in that valley, I didn't know what to do. My mind got all confused.

We lose what we don't repeatedly use!

This scenario applies to EVERYTHING… our biking, our relationships, our nutrition, our education, our work performance, and most importantly our walk with God.

You can have tons of church experience. You can have a fancy Bible with your name on it. None of it matters if you're not consistent. Small things consistently done produce great results! What you do every day matters more than what you do every once and a while. Part-time faith will NEVER produce full-time blessings!

*   *   *

"We know that in all things God works for the good of those who love him, who have been called according to his purpose." Romans 8:28

*   *   *

How much time do you spend with God each day?

_____

_____

_____

_____

Explain a time when you have been guilty of part-time faith.

_____

_____

_____

_____

_____

_____

_____

What are you doing to strengthen your relationship with Jesus?

_____

_____

_____

_____

_____

_____

How can you help others get their mojo back with God?

_____

_____

_____

_____

_____

_____

Day #7

Ice Cream and Coffee

Y'all, I'm tired.

And I don't quite think sleeping in, taking a nap, or going to bed any earlier is gonna fix it.

I'm tired of the mainstream media.

I'm tired of political "parties". Nothing about it is a party.

I'm tired of the snide remarks and disrespectful comments.

I'm tired of the lack of kindness.

I'm tired of conspiracy theories and fake news.

I'm tired of people politicizing both religion and science.

I'm tired of picking sides.

I'm tired of social distancing.

I'm tired of no one wanting to work.

I'm tired of mixed messages and crazy state mandates.

I'm tired of the fact-checkers and all their warning labels.

I'm tired of hidden agendas and a lack of transparency.

I'm tired of not knowing the outcome.

I'm tired of fearing the worst.

I'm tired of all of it.

I'm just tired.

So, I'm having my favorite ice cream for breakfast this morning... yep, right outta the carton. Ice cream and coffee... yum. Don't judge! This is emotional eating at its best because whiskey before work is frowned upon.

Y'all, I'm tired—not crazy.

*   *   *

"Then Jesus said, "Come to me, all who are weary and carry heavy burdens, and I will give you rest." Matthew 11:28

*   *   *

What makes you tired these days?

_____

_____

_____

_____

_____

_____

_____

How do you keep a positive spirit?

_____

_____

_____

_____

_____

_____

_____

What is your "ice cream for breakfast?"

_____

_____

_____

_____

_____

_____

_____

Week Eleven

Starting Over

Starting over is definitely one of those bittersweet moments. In order to start over, it means something else had to end. And, usually, that something else was pretty important. But, the sky truly is the limit when we start over. It's the ultimate second chance at getting it right… and this time you've got experience on your side. You've also got God.

> *Dear Lord, give me strength to start again. Fill me with patience and perseverance. Help me stay focused. Don't allow me to settle for less than my best. Let this time be my best time. In Jesus's name, Amen.*

PRAYER JOURNAL

Who will you pray for this week? What situations need God's guidance? Where does Jesus need to intervene? How can the Holy Spirit help? Date it and state it! Pray for these things each day this week. Update it as needed.

Day #1

Do Over!

Today's goal: Don't be afraid to start over!

We all make mistakes. We all fall short, and we all fail miserably at something. That's life. You dust yourself off and try again. That's much easier said than done, right? But, I know a few things about starting over.

I'm now living in my third city when I thought I'd never leave my hometown. I spent 13 years working at one middle school only to be on year number 13 at another one. And, after spending 15 years on my first marriage, I'm 32 blissful years into my second one. And, don't forget my children. They're 29, 24, and 12. Talk about starting over! Then there's my 427th attempt at dieting, my 10th new hair color, my 3rd new car, and my 2nd camper. And, on a more serious note, there's life after spending time in a mental health facility battling depression and then there's trying to find a new normal after losing my only brother. At this point, I consider myself an expert at starting over, but I think it's a BEAUTIFUL thing, folks.

Do you remember playing four-square or badminton in PE? What would you shout to the group when you messed up? "Do over!" And, wasn't that THE BEST feeling—a second chance at getting it right? When did starting over become so scary (or embarrassing)? It happened once we started placing more value on the world's reaction vs. God's amazing grace. But, it's NEVER too late—Moses, Job, Gideon, Paul, Esther, Ruth—the Bible is filled with people who needed a fresh start.

"I hope you live a life you're proud of, and if you find you're not, I hope you have the strength to start over."

Remember: There's a big difference between giving up and starting over! You're no longer starting from scratch; you're starting from experience.

And, if you've been blessed enough to avoid a re-do, know this: change is hard… whether it happens on New Year's Day, a birthday, the first day of school, or right in the middle of a hectic work week. Don't be a discourager; be a cheerleader! Trust me. They're already filled with enough guilt. They need your grace. Grace is the face love wears when it meets imperfection.

*   *   *

"But forget all that— it is nothing compared to what I am going to do." Isaiah 43:18

*   *   *

What area of your life would you most desire a re-do AND why?

_____

_____

_____

_____

_____

_____

What's keeping you from starting over?

_____

_____

_____

_____

_____

_____

_____

Day #2

Never Too Broken

So, I recently hiked Providence Canyon with my baby boy. It's also known as Georgia's "Little Grand Canyon." This beautiful place was caused by bad farming practices during the 1800s. Ain't that kinda wild?!? Bad agricultural practices created both massive erosion of the Coastal Plain AND a beautiful masterpiece.

It reminds me of the time I got pregnant in high school. Talk about a terrible mistake! But, that very negative situation turned into one of my all-time greatest blessings. That baby boy taught me so much about life, motherhood, and becoming who you want to be, not who you've been.

It also reminds me of the time I had to take an extended leave from work—right slap dab in the middle of the school year—to battle depression in a mental health facility. Man, talk about some bad timing! But, God became my best friend while I was there. Our relationship was pretty nonexistent until that moment, when he saved me from drowning.

I'm starting to see a pattern here—are you?

God uses—bad practices, bad mistakes, bad situations, and bad timing—and turns them into something good. No mistake is too big and no past is too bad! There's no such thing as "too far gone" with God. I'm living proof.

> Today's Lesson: You are never too broken to be repaired by God!

Amy Bowdoin

*   *   *

*"Though we are overwhelmed by our sins,
you forgive them all." Psalm 65:3*

*   *   *

When was a time you felt "too far gone" with God?

_____

_____

_____

_____

_____

_____

How did God use your brokenness?

_____

_____

_____

_____

_____

_____

How have you helped other broken people experience God's unfailing love?

_____

_____

_____

_____

_____

_____

_____

Day #3

Stop Looking

When my baby boy was about six years old, he was walking across a boat dock to join me on a four-wheeler when a tiny nightmare occurred. Tons of wasps flew out from under the dock and started nailing him—on the neck, the cheek, the forehead, etc... It was awful! Naturally, he was upset and I was, too. Were all the stings to the head more dangerous? Could he be allergic? Fortunately, we both survived the traumatic experience... kinda.

He recovered physically, but mentally he had hit a roadblock. He was now terrified of wasps and yellow jackets. And, when I say terrified, I mean terrified. Initially, his fears were warranted. His pain (from the stings) was still too real. But then, six turned to seven, seven turned to eight, and he could not let it go—he could not get over what had happened. We tried everything to ease his mind. Prayers. Avoidance. Bug spray. Bribery. Nothing worked.

So, imagine my surprise to discover yesterday afternoon that wasps no longer bothered him. Say what?!?! And, that's when my soon-to-be ten year old preached right to my heart.

"Mama, I've been scared of bees my whole life, and I'm tired of being scared. So, I came up with a strategy and it's working."

"What's that?"

"It's simple. I stopped looking for them."

"What?"

"When you spend your time looking for bad things, you're going to find them. So, I stopped looking for them and started looking for the good. And, it's working."

I was so moved by what he said that I wanted to share his strategy with you. Surely I'm not the only one guilty of losing my focus?!? I pride myself in being a positive person, but sometimes all I see are bad decisions, missed opportunities, and where I (and others) fall short. And, there are other times when it's REALLY hard for me to let some things go. All of this weighs me down and keeps me from being who God created me to be. It's time I start looking for the good in my life. Join me! We will look adorable in our rose-colored glasses. Just remember: It's not what you look for that matters; it's what you see! See the good.

*   *   *

"... The Lord doesn't see things the way you see them. People judge by outward appearance, but the Lord looks at the heart." 1 Samual 16:7

*   *   *

What are you always looking for?

_____

_____

_____

_____

_____

_____

_____

What do you need to stop seeing?

_____

_____

_____

_____

_____

_____

How can a change in perspective help you "start over?"

_____

_____

_____

_____

_____

_____

Day #4

BUT GOD!

I have two grown children. One is 29 years old, has lived in Philadelphia for about ten years, and is currently using his health policy degree to solve all our insurance and pharmaceutical problems. The other one is 24 years old, is happily married, and flips houses and sells cars like he's done it his whole life. I'm super proud of both of them. Mission accomplished, Momma!

So, I should be done, folks—an empty nester eating bonbons and binge watching Netflix. But, I'm not because I'm also the momma of an active 12 year old boy. I used to laugh at God's sense of humor for making me start over, but now I realize He actually blessed me more than I deserved.

That little boy loves his momma big! I know this because he (repeatedly) tells me and confesses it on post-it notes around the house. He always holds my hand and asks me about my day on our car ride home. He's my copilot and my partner in crime, and he makes me laugh just like his daddy. He's the sweetest thing that's ever been mine, and he's currently babbling about drum beats as I write this post.

I NEVER imagined having a 3rd child—like never ever. I fully anticipated cruising gracefully to the finish line.

BUT, GOD.

He had different plans for me. Plans to shake things up in such a way that I had to start completely over. And, not just a little bit over, but new town, new job, new house, new spouse kinda over.

I can still remember those sleepless nights when I first brought him home. I even remember questioning, "What am I doing here?" Because when you think you're done (having babies), a do-over is quite shocking. Little did I know what God had in store for me.

I darn sure didn't understand it at the time, but it sure does make beautiful sense now.

Thank you, Lord, for your unexpected blessings. Even when we don't ask, you are always faithful and on time. You fulfill our every need— even those we didn't realize we needed. Amen!

If you're currently confused about something, your clarity is coming. Sometimes what we're looking for comes when we're not looking at all.

I thought I was done... BUT GOD!

*   *   *

[Jesus replied, "You don't understand now what I am doing, but someday you will." John 13:7]

*   *   *

What is your BUT GOD moment?

_____

_____

_____

_____

_____

_____

Describe a time when you had to start over.

_____

_____

_____

_____

_____

_____

_____

Where do you still need clarity from God?

_____

_____

_____

_____

_____

_____

_____

Day #5

Rise Again

We all have that one Bible verse that speaks to us more than the others.

Well, Micah 7:8 is mine. When I say this verse, I can hear the theme song to "Rocky" playing in my mind. It's my verse, y'all.

But, you can't really appreciate it unless you've been broken. And, I have. I face-planted so hard onto rock bottom that I saw the basement, folks. It cost me some friends, one husband, my reputation, and my joy. But, there's beauty in hitting rock bottom, and it's called clarity.

It became quite clear who was in my tribe and who had only been along for the ride. It also became quite clear who believed everything they heard and who believed in me. But, even worse than all that, was losing myself in the chaos. My joy. My hope. My faith. It was all gone. I was an empty vessel, damaged goods, a shell of the woman I had been before, but guess what? He still wanted me. After all I had done, He still chose me.

Oh, the overwhelming, never-ending, reckless love of God!

Storms suck. But, It took that storm for me to see how badly I needed Jesus, and that experience changed my life, folks.

We recently had some storms here in Georgia. It's never fun when they happen during the night. For the majority of us, it's back to reality today. A few broken limbs, some down lines, a night without power. It's all good. We'll be fully recovered and shouting, "TGIF!" by lunchtime. But, we have some friends who are still battling some major storms this morning: depression, defeat, grief, doubt, divorce, etc... Love on them. Pray for them. Encourage them. Loan them some of your strength and perseverance if you have to. Whatever it takes. BECAUSE THAT'S WHAT TRUE FRIENDS DO! And, I can promise you this, when they rise again (and they will), your loyalty will be remembered.

*   *   *

*"Do not gloat over my troubles. Though I
have fallen, I will RISE AGAIN!
Though I sit in darkness, the Lord will be my light." Micah 7:8*

*   *   *

Share a time when you've been broken.

_____

_____

_____

_____

_____

_____

Who helped you during this time?

_____

What did their help mean to you?

_____

_____

_____

How can you help your discouraged friends right now?

_____

_____

_____

_____

_____

_____

_____

How can you RISE AGAIN?

_____

_____

_____

_____

_____

_____

_____

Day #6

OUCH!

We recently had to put down one of our pets. I had never been on the losing side of loving a pet before. Unfortunately, it took losing one to make me appreciate the one left behind. Knox has now gone from the outhouse to the penthouse, folks. He sleeps on this plush bed in our bedroom, we take him on all our camping trips, and now he's doing life right along with us (as he should have been from the beginning). He might be big, but he's a total cuddle bug. In fact, he demands lots of heavy petting and snuggles. He's part boxer, so maybe that's where he gets it. But, he will reach out, much like a handshake, to get your attention. And, when I say this is his trademark, it really is. He does it all the time.

Well, yesterday I was lying across our chair relaxing when here he comes, tail just a-wagging. I gave him a good rub down, but he wanted more. So, he did what he always does—he reached out to get my attention. But, what he got was my chin.

"OUCH, KNOX!!!!!"

And, in classic fashion, he just looked at me... so sweet, so genuine, and so sorry for hurting me. And, while it was a total accident, it still hurt. And, it left me with a big decision to make. Do I forgive him or do I make him suffer indefinitely for what he's done?

But, here's the deal, folks. (And, I need you to really sit up straight when you read this next line.)

Love hurts sometimes.

And, it's usually the people we love the most who do the hurtin'. But, don't let one little mistake cause you to forget ALL the things they've done right. Life is too short for that nonsense.

My grandmother also told me something else, "Some people are worth a second chance." But, you'll never heal until you forgive them. Remember that.

*   *   *

"Love is not self-seeking. It is not easily angered. It keeps no record of wrongdoing." 1 Corinthians 13:5

*   *   *

Who in your life needs a second chance?

_____

_____

_____

_____

_____

_____

What's preventing you from giving them another shot?

_____

_____

_____

_____

_____

_____

What's the best way to heal broken hearts and rebuild burnt bridges?

_____

_____

_____

_____

_____

_____

_____

Day #7

One Small Thing

I'm not real sure when it happened.

After my divorce? Probably.

After enduring depression? Perhaps.

After starting over? Yes.

After a few failures? Maybe.

After some disappointments? Possibly.

After a friend was two-faced? For sure.

After I let myself down? Absolutely.

After I suffered a loss? Oh, yes.

After I reached a goal? Definitely.

After I tried something new? It's likely.

After I met my BFFs? For real tho!

I'm not the same person who started this journey over 46 years ago. Heck, I'm not even the same person from last year. Life changes you. Events change you. People change you. Circumstances change you. Politics and pandemics change you. But, I wouldn't want it any other way. Change is where the magic happens!

Repeat after me: I can do ALL things!

I can even do really difficult things… like pedaling up a ginormous hill at Fort Yargo State Park. It would have been a fairly easy task had it been mile one or two on a cool fall day. But, this was mile 8.5 on a blazing hot day. The old me would have quit and walked my bike to the top. But, the new me welcomes the chance to practice determination and perseverance. And, while it's a minor, insignificant change, it's a change, folks.

Goal: Change one small thing today and bigger changes will follow. (And, if all you change today is your underwear, well, that's a start. Ha.)

We were not put on this earth to remain stagnant. We are here to grow, to evolve, to change. Don't fear the process. Fear being in the exact same place next year as you are right now.

*   *   *

"Turn to God and change the way you think and
act because the kingdom of heaven is near."
Matthew 3:2

*   *   *

What is something you need to change? Why?

_____

_____

_____

_____

_____

_____

_____

How will you make this happen?

_____

_____

_____

_____

_____

_____

_____

_____

Week Twelve

Revival

When I was very young, Tabernacle Baptist Church would host a revival each year. The congregation would gather nightly—for a solid week—to hear sermons from various preachers. It was meant to rejuvenate a tired spirit. It was meant to light a fire in the church. But, churches don't host week-long revivals anymore. Why? Probably because so many of us claim to be too busy. When in reality, our priorities are screwed up. It's more important for Mike and Mary to attend their sports practice than church. Ouch! But, a spiritual revival is exactly what you need. It starts on the inside and overflows into everything you see, do, think, and speak.

You can do all the things:

- You can let go of what weighs you down
- You can awaken to things that bring you joy
- You can breathe fresh air on hikes with your girlfriends
- You can hold on to your mustard seeds of faith
- You can ignore the noise of the world
- You can find your balance
- You can be brave enough to start over
- You can even strive to be that girl.

But, if you don't have a heart for Jesus, if you're not on fire for Jesus, if you're not chasing him from the inside-out, then none of this even matters.

*Dear Lord, light a fire in my heart and let it burn…
all the guilt and all the regret. Let it burn what's
weighing me down and keeping me from living my
best life. Let it burn the negative thoughts I play on
repeat. Let it burn my insecurities, my doubts, and
my fears. Use the ashes to mold me into who you
have created me to be—fearfully and wonderfully
made, strong and courageous. I can do all things.
I am the daughter of the one true king. In Jesus's
name, Amen.*

PRAYER JOURNAL

Who will you pray for this week? What situations need God's guidance? Where does Jesus need to intervene? How can the Holy Spirit help? Date it and state it! Pray for these things each day this week. Update it as needed.

Day #1

The Appreciation Box

I try not to write too much about my work because that's usually frowned upon. But, yesterday, something so incredibly precious happened that I must share it with the world.

We got another new student last week. But, this one speaks zero English. She's from Honduras, and she is super adorable—the kinda adorable that belongs on the front of a magazine. But, this child is different. She's hungry for knowledge, and she's learning more and more every day. Her discipline and work ethic are unmatched. She's only been in my classroom one week, and she's already won my heart.

During the morning announcements yesterday, she proudly stood with her hand on her heart for the Pledge, but she remained silent—not out of defiance, not to protest a cause, but because she genuinely did not know the words. Immediately when it was over, she ran up to me with her translator app opened on her phone. She handed it to me, and it read, "Please give me those words. I want to learn it." So, we pulled up the Pledge on my computer. She took a pic of it with her phone and walked back to her seat filled with pride and hope. Not only could you see it on her face, but you could feel it oozing outta her pores. That's the good stuff, folks.

But, it reminded me of a sermon from Andy Stanley. He had two boxes on the table. One was titled "appreciation" and the other one was titled "expectation." He preached an entire sermon about the importance of keeping things in our appreciation box.

Dinner on the table… appreciated.

Clean clothes… appreciated.

Fresh cut grass… appreciated.

Hard days work… appreciated.

But, it's when we put those items in the other box that we run into trouble.

It's when dinner becomes expected that a husband becomes angry when it's not ready and waiting for him. It's when a good looking lawn becomes expected that a wife pitches a fit when the curb appeal is lacking. You get the idea.

We no longer appreciate it because we now expect it.

Many Americans are living outta the wrong box these days. We expect cheaper gas prices, better service, stocked grocery shelves, a good education, free speech, etc… and because we expect it, we no longer appreciate how good we have it. And, we darn sure don't appreciate the sacrifices it took to get it. I see it every day in my classroom, at the grocery, and even at church. We've been spoiled, and that has turned several of us into apathetic brats— myself included—just a big ol' bunch of entitled complainers with 1st world problems.

But, not this new little girl. She's a sponge, soaking it all in and savoring every single minute of it. She's not taking any of it for granted. She is so proud to be in America, and it shows.

We live in the greatest country in the world. We don't need new laws, crazy mandates, or tax credits to make it better. We need a spiritual revival! We also need Jesus and a grateful heart.

*   *   *

You should remember the words of the Lord Jesus: 'It is more blessed to give than to receive." Acts 20:35

*   *   *

Where do you need to experience a revival in your life?

_____

_____

_____

_____

_____

_____

_____

What do you need to move from the expectation box to the appreciation box?

EXPECTATION	APPRECIATION

Day #2

Not "Just a Thursday"

It was just a Thursday morning. I was home from the gym and racing to the shower. That's when I heard it—a loud boom. I thought it was my hubby dropping something in the kitchen, so I kept rushing through my regular routine. It would be a few minutes later before I realized what I had really heard.

Outside my house, in my front yard, two vehicles collided head on. It looked like a scene from a movie, but this was no dress rehearsal. All the red and blue flashing lights seemed so pretty against the dark morning sky, but in reality, I was witnessing a nightmare. All the first responders were racing around like determined ants. The man who crashed into our fence was trapped inside his vehicle. The other man was on the ground. Both the driver's side of each vehicle had been demolished—shredded and crushed like an aluminum can.

It would be a few minutes later before I learned the man trapped inside his vehicle had died—right there in my front yard. My heart hurt for this man I never knew; it still hurts.

Did he kiss his wife before he left?

Did he hug his children on his way out the door?

When was the last time he called his mama?

Did he know Jesus?

Fast forward to that afternoon. Bill and I were working in our camper, and that's when the first truck pulled up. Two men stepped outside. It was the deceased man's father and grandfather. They wanted to see—they needed to see—where he had taken his last breath. Bill and I learned he was only 32 years old, he had an eleven-year-old son, he was on his way to work that morning, and he was the only child of the man standing in our yard. My heart sank even further hearing this news. We also learned the wreck was not his fault. The other man had fallen asleep at the wheel and crossed the yellow line, and as a result, a life had ended—unplanned, without notice, and too soon.

It was just a Thursday, right? Wrong.

It wasn't just a Thursday. It was his LAST Thursday. Had he known, I'm sure he would have hugged a little longer, kissed a little slower, called his mama one more time, and stopped putting off some dreams he had for himself. But, he thought he had more time, which is something we are all guilty of assuming.

As I was churning all this over in my mind, a second truck pulled up. It was a big brown box truck with a package just for me. It was from Camping World. It was their olive branch of peace after an unfortunate incident happened during the purchase of our first camper. Inside the box of goodies was a handwritten note—a gentle reminder that God knew I needed. It ended with, "We travel not to escape life, but for life not to escape us." Amen!

Today is not "just another day". This is the day the Lord has made! It is your chance to be fearless in the pursuit of what sets your soul on fire. Don't wait to be happy. Go create it! Why? Because sometimes 'later' becomes 'never'.

You will never have this day again. Do what makes you feel alive.

Chase after it like it's a full time job. I do.

*   *   *

"This is the day the Lord has made. We will rejoice and be glad in it." Psalm 118:24

*   *   *

How will you make today count?

_____
_____
_____
_____
_____
_____
_____

I've asked the above question before. How do you stop writing about it and dreaming about it, and put it into action? What in the world are you waiting for?

_____
_____
_____
_____
_____
_____
_____

What would you do if you knew it was your "last Thursday?"

_____

_____

_____

_____

_____

_____

_____

Day #3

Reminder: Pray

I absolutely loved my Fitbit watch. It lasted about 4 years, and then it kicked the bucket. That's when I upgraded myself to one of those fancy Apple watches. I've had it about a year now, and I've grown quite fond of it. Actually, I won't leave home without it. It is one tracking machine, folks... steps, miles, calories, my sleep, etc... It keeps up with all of it. But, one of my favorite features is the gentle reminder to stand up.

The watch expects me to stand (for a few minutes) each hour I'm awake. Most hours I do this naturally, walking to the restroom or refilling my water. But, it catches me slackin' on a few. I'm vegging on the coach, my watch vibrates, and I read what it says, "Girl, you need to stand up." So, I comply and my watch vibrates again. "Congratulations! You did it!" It's an awesome feature—much like a cattle prod. Well, I decided to start using that feature for something else: my prayers.

Y'all know our days can get crazy chaotic and life will run away with us if we let it. So now, when my watch vibrates, I pretend it's saying, "Girl, you need to pray." It's never anything elaborate, or fancy, or planned out. It's just me and Jesus and a simple conversation among friends.

"Hey. It's me—Amy. I'm just checking in again. You know I was kidding when I said that ugly word, right? I'm here to be a blessing if you need me. Talk soon. Amen."

"Hey. It's me—Amy. I'm struggling with doubt today. It stinks. I could use some extra joy. Talk soon. Amen."

"Hey. It's me—Amy. I sure do appreciate the sunshine. Thanks for being there. Talk soon. Amen."

"Hey. It's me—Amy. Can you believe that heifer? She really gets on my nerves. Help! Talk soon. Amen."

"Hey. It's me—Amy. Today's been a pretty good day. I know it's because of you. Thank you. Talk soon. Amen."

Guys, this has been a big game changer for me. I always say my prayers in the morning, when I'm most awake and my house is still quiet. But, I honestly don't think a lot about it during the day. How can I have a personal relationship with Jesus if I never share the little things with him? I can't. This gentle nudge on my wrist has remedied that. I talk to Jesus all day long, and my life is fuller because of it.

If you have an Apple Watch, consider joining me. If you don't, pick something else… like praying at stop signs, or railroad crossings, or during commercials, or every time you pass a Dollar General. "Prayer does not help our relationship with God. Prayer IS our relationship with God."

*   *   *

"Look to the Lord and his strength; seek his face… always." 1 Chronicles 16:11

*   *   *

When do you typically say your prayers?

Do you ever find yourself "praying on repeat" or just going through the motions?

_____

_____

_____

_____

_____

_____

What can you do to ensure you pray more often?

_____

_____

_____

_____

_____

_____

What reminders can you use…

_____

_____

_____

_____

_____

_____

Day #4

Still in Training

I need to brag on my baby boy. I'm also carving this in stone, so I don't forget his inner goodness after he hits his teenage years.

On our last visit to Tugaloo State Park, I wanted to buy a sweatshirt from the park office, so he went inside with me. As we were leaving, I walked outside the door. I noticed an older woman approaching, but I thought nothing of it. She was still a ways away. When I looked back to make sure my kid was in tow, he wasn't there. I turned further around, and that's when I noticed it.

He had stopped to hold open the door for this woman. She said the obligatory thank you, and he said, "Have a nice day, ma'am." My heart swelled with pride.

Y'all, I have done a lot of things wrong—terribly wrong. But, I'm getting this one right. Thank you, Jesus!

But, it's baby steps. One spring and summer we practiced shaking hands and looking folks dead in the eye. He was a nervous wreck when he started this lesson. Now, he's a trained professional.

He definitely learned the art of appreciation from his daddy. He says thank you for EVERYTHING. Just last night, his dad played a racing game with him. When they were done, he said, "Thanks so much, Dad, for playing with me. I loved it." He might be spoiled, but how can you not spoil a child who oozes with genuine appreciation?

Over the Christmas holidays, he learned another nonnegotiable: you must always remove your hat for the Pledge, the National Anthem, and the blessing. I'm kinda shocked how many people have forgotten this.

And, when it comes to the blessing, the time for reciting cute rhymes is over. We started this lesson in 4th grade. You speak from the heart when talking to the Lord. I'll admit there was an awkward silence at first. He had no idea what to say. But, now, he'd give Andy Stanley a run for his money.

To say I'm proud of this child, is an understatement. He's super smart, observant, and genuine. But, more than all that, he's a good human. Compassionate. Honest and kind. He didn't start that way. It took daily practice and coaching.

Guys, that's why it's soooooo important that we stay in God's word. The Bible is filled with life lessons and hope. When life gets messy and difficult, it's our lifeline. When life gets overwhelming and complicated, it's our anchor. We know these things to be true, yet many times we use it as a last resort.

My mama loves to say, "I taught you better than that." It's usually stated after she catches me with my elbows on the table. But, can you imagine Jesus saying the same thing?

Oh, ye of little faith! Get it together. Turn off the news and open up that Bible. You're still in training.

Lesson: If we don't teach our children to follow Christ, the world will teach them not to.

*   *   *

"Train up a child in the way he should go; even when he is old he will not depart from it." Proverbs 22:6

*   *   *

When it comes to your life, in what areas are you still "in training?"

_____
_____
_____
_____
_____
_____

How much time do you spend watching television vs. reading your Bible?

_____

How much time do you spend scrolling social media vs. reading your Bible?

_____

Is this a number that makes you proud?

_____

What priorities are you modeling for your children/grandchildren?

_____
_____
_____
_____
_____

Day #5

Don't Stay in the Boat

Y'all, I am 100% convinced that God works in mysterious ways and nothing—and I do mean nothing—is left to chance.

I shared the other week how a friend gave me an old book that smells like mothballs. I'm slowly plugging away at it, and it continues to be exactly what I need to hear. I never even knew this book existed until God placed it on her heart to share it with me... and she answered that call. Guys, that's HUGE!!! That's faith in action, and the world kinda needs more of that.

Well, there's a mind-blowing section in that book about unanswered prayers. The author's mother poured her heart out to God for a dollar—a single dollarM—and nothing. That unanswered prayer made her doubt her faith and question God. During that time, she was living with a pastor and his family for a revival. The pastor kept receiving love offerings and would never share it—not even a dollar. Several months passed before a mutual friend cleared up the confusion.

God heard her mother's prayers, and He placed it on the preacher's heart to give her a dollar. But, the flesh is weak! Before he could act, the devil planted seeds of greed and doubt. The preacher even confessed, "She's better off than me. She doesn't need my dollar." So, he kept it. He didn't answer God's call. And, guys, that's HUGE, too!

God is never gonna have money fall from the sky, through our sunroof, and into our purse. He simply doesn't work that way. He uses His people. That's what it means (to me) to be the "hands and feet of God."

"Many will be called but few are chosen," should be "Many will be called but few actually answer." (Let that sink in a minute, folks.)

This is why it's so important for us to be "noticers". When God places something on our heart, it's there on purpose. Don't deny it. Don't delay it. Act on it!

Last Sunday morning I prayed over a box of 8 notecards. "Dear Lord, who needs to know they're loved and valued this week?" And, one by one, names came to mind. Random names, guys. A few I haven't spoken to in months. I put all 8 cards in my mailbox Sunday night. Well, imagine my surprise Monday morning when I happened to bump into one of those people. We were stuck between the wall and the 6th grade copier.

"Are you okay? I hate to see people stuck."

And, right there, folks, she started confessing how overwhelmed she felt. She was visibly upset and crying. And I thought, "Dear God, she has no idea there's a card filled with affirmation just for her in my mailbox at this very moment. You are incredible!"

But, guys, faith in action causes a tremendous domino effect. God put her name on my heart. I answered that call, but it wasn't just her who was blessed. That encounter strengthened my own faith. I've been quite complacent lately when it comes to acknowledging what God is asking me to do. I'm guilty of being just like that preacher. But, ever since I started acting on that nudge, I have felt God moving in my life more than ever before. It is the most indescribable feeling. And, I want that for you, too.

"You don't have faith and wait. When you have faith, you move." Please don't stay in the boat when God is calling you to walk on water.

*   *   *

"When they call on me, I will answer. I will be with them in times of trouble. I will rescue and honor them." Psalm 91:15

*   *   *

Describe a time when you were stuck.

_____

_____

_____

_____

_____

_____

Who noticed?

_____

Who do you know who is stuck right now?

_____

_____

_____

_____

_____

_____

How can you lighten their load?

_____

_____

_____

_____

_____

_____

_____

Why is answering God's call so important?

_____

_____

_____

_____

_____

_____

_____

Day #6

Everyone

Good morning, sinners.

I'm the world's worst, too. I smack my gum. I overindulge in Fireball Whisky. I talk about others, and I hold grudges to the grave. I also lie, but about sweet things like Santa Claus, the Easter Bunny, and that your new haircut looks great. But, we've all done that, right? Right? Please tell me I'm not the only one.

But, you wanna know what I'm really good at? Pointing out imperfections in others. She's a gossip. He's a crook. They're both moochers! She only lives like that on Sunday morning. What a fake! And, it's those fakers who make me cuss a little. Those heifers who play the victim to the storms they created. I can't take that mess at all, and it's cost me friendships. But, when I do this, when I get all agitated, disgruntled, and holier than thou, the devil wins. Because, if I'm so focused on their sins, there's no time to pray (and work) on mine.

We're currently living in a world where everyone has an opinion, everyone's an expert, and everyone is always right. I need "everyone" to use those skills to further God's kingdom—not divide us even further. We all fall short, but what we don't all do is admit it. It's time for a little self-reflection, folks. In the words of Michael Jackson, "If you wanna make the world a better place, take a look at yourself and then make a change."

Amy Bowdoin

*   *   *

"Why do you see the speck that is in your friend's eye, but do not notice the log that is in your own?" Matthew 7:3

*   *   *

On a scale of 1 to 10, how judgemental are you?

_____

How often do you admit when you are wrong?

_____
_____
_____
_____
_____
_____

Why, as Christians, are we so quick to point out the flaws in others?

_____
_____
_____
_____
_____
_____

How do we break this bad habit?

_____

_____

_____

_____

_____

_____

When it comes to self-improvement, what are you currently working on/praying for?

_____

_____

_____

_____

_____

_____

Day #7

Change Starts at Home

I'm a teacher, and I've been one for twenty-five years. The grade level doesn't matter. The subject doesn't matter. Why? Because I'm a teacher, and teachers are born with a gene that allows us to love ALL people. I'm sure you've heard someone say, "Once you're my student, you're my kid for life." And, it's true.

Well, about 13 years ago, I had the pleasure of being an "academic coach" to a select group of student-athletes. My job was to encourage them, support them, love them, and hold them accountable. We made a great team. These guys met me an hour before school started (each day) to hit the books. We also met once a week over the summer to keep our minds sharp and our behavior in check. It was a labor of love, and we were invested in each other. As incentives, we had t-shirts made and attended school-sponsored field trips. It was a fantastic program. But, I'll never forget one certain trip. It was to a skating rink in Newnan, Georgia.

The requirement to attend was to have zero discipline referrals and all As and Bs. About ten boys qualified for the trip, so my husband-at-the-time (yes, you read that right) and I carpooled them to the skating rink. It was their very first time attempting to skate, so naturally I had my camera ready. All the music, laughter, and smiles were fantastic, but that soon ended. I couldn't find my pocketbook. Silly me! We all searched for it and finally found it thrown in a corner. What in the world? As I looked inside, things were missing, including my camera. We immediately located the manager who immediately got the owner. I needed these two (white) men to react and quickly, but what transpired next was awful. They were very condescending and belittling to me. Why? Because my boys weren't just any boys, they were black boys.

"M'am, we're not calling the police. We're certain one of 'those' boys did this."

"Which boys? Not my boys! I need you to call the police or start questioning your customers."

"M'am, we see it all the time. People like yourself bring these type of kids in here, and they're the very ones doing the stealing."

"First of all, these boys earned this trip by excelling in academics and behavior. These boys are kind and honest and would never steal from anyone."

"M'am, until we search these boys, we're not looking any further. We know one of them did it."

I'm leaving out a chunk of this nasty conversation, but what you need to know is "those boys" were standing behind me and witnessing all of this. The owner even said, "One of you boys need to confess, so we can get back to business." I was at a loss, and my heart hurt for my boys. Their evening—their much deserved evening—had been ruined. But, that's when one of them stepped forward. I'll never forget it. With his arms stretched out like Jesus on the cross, he said, "You can search me. I don't steal, and I'd never hurt my teacher. I love her like a mom." And, one by one, they each followed suit. Nothing! Absolutely nothing! They were not the guilty ones. That joker cut bait and walked to the bowling alley once he smelled trouble.

Once we received the "all clear" from the owner, he called the police. A (white) deputy sheriff arrived on the scene, and he was phenomenal. He took our information and apologized to my boys. He even said he had a good hunch who did it. How is that even possible? Because the manager, the owner, and the entire police force all knew the shady local kid who was always causing trouble. Fortunately for me, that shady kid wasn't too smart. He returned to the skating rink with my camera the very next night. I was asked to come to the police station to claim my things. They had the juvenile delinquent in custody waiting to see if I wanted to press charges. That's crazy, right? He stole everything outta my pocketbook and ruined our entire field trip, but they're waiting. Is that protocol with minors? I have no idea. Or, was it because the guilty culprit was a white boy? I'll never know, but you better believe my answer was… HELL YES!!!

I got my pictures developed the next day. There were some great ones of my guys and a few of "him." He could have been the poster child for white trash… no shirt, multiple rebel flags, and shooting birds at the camera. That poor child needed my prayers and some Jesus. And, while this has been a super long post, I need you to pay close attention to this next part. It's the most important part.

As my boys were piling out of my car, I kept apologizing for their ruined evening and how they were treated. I was hurt, frustrated, and angry that anyone would treat them so hatefully. They were good boys. And that's when they said it… "It's okay. This happens to us ALL THE TIME!" All the time?!? Let that sink in, folks. I am forty-five years old, and I've experienced racism one time. One time, and it was with them, and it was vile and ugly and degrading and inhumane. And, until you're in that moment and witness someone you love being mistreated because of their brown skin, you'll never understand the magnitude of the moment we're in right now.

We've been redoing my youngest son's bedroom, so we've had plenty of time to talk about current events. He made an innocent comment yesterday that made my mommy heart ooze with pride. He has a couple of stuffed animals that he likes to sleep with at night. He was trying to arrange them on his bed when he said, "I don't know why, but I feel really bad when I treat them differently." I quickly responded, "I know why. You have a good heart, and I hope you always feel that way… about your stuffed animals, your friends, your coworkers, and your neighbors." We need change, folks, but we'll never find it rioting or looting. We will, however, find it at home. Some folks are convinced that racism is taught, but so is kindness, compassion, generosity, and love. Especially love. That stuff is homemade. So, while I'm not marching in streets or reposting controversial videos, I am doing my part. Boys who are held to high standards by their mom will one day hold high standards for themselves. "It's not my job to toughen up my son to face a cruel and heartless world. It is my job to raise a son who will make the world less cruel and heartless."

*   *   *

"Come, follow Me," Jesus said, "and I will make you fishers of men." Matthew 4:19

*   *   *

What lessons have been taught in your home?

_____

_____

_____

_____

_____

_____

How are you helping create a more positive climate in your community?

_____

_____

_____

_____

_____

_____

The world needs braver Christians. How can you share your love for Jesus with others?

_____

_____

_____

_____

_____

_____

_____

Now What?

It's definitely true what they say: All good things must come to an end. Our 12 weeks together is now over. In my best Jesus voice, "It is finished." Ha. But, now what? How do you take this devotional and apply it to your life? You take it one day at a time. That's how.

So many times, we try to be everything to everybody. That mess is exhausting, folks. And, we end up losing ourselves in the process. Trust me.

I can do *some* things fairly well, but I can't do *all* things worth a darn. So, I must prioritize my focus. One day I will focus on my relationships. I'm gonna pour into others—my friends and family—like it's a full time job. The next day I'm gonna pour into myself. The following day I might work on cleaning the house and my heart (And, if I'm honest, that might just take two days). Every day has its own focus, BUT **every day begins and ends with Jesus**.

We have this notion that our spiritual time must be formal and super serious. That's insane thinking. Jesus wants an intimate relationship with you. He wants the banter you give your best friends over chips and salsa and Margaritas. You know when the conversation is real— well, so does Jesus. Your time with Jesus might look like tears in the shower or jamming to a song on your way to work. It might look like a quiet moment hiding in the bathroom with the Oreos, or it might be taking a breath of fresh air after a much needed hike. This time with Jesus—twice a day—**will** change your life. So, now what? Well, that's up to you, isn't it?

CPSIA information can be obtained
at www.ICGtesting.com
Printed in the USA
JSHW011539150223
37714JS00004B/16